Bad Moon Rising

A Study in the Book of Revelation

Rev. Derek Craig Jones

There is a storm rising out of the east. It is not a secret or a surprise to those who have ears to hear and eyes to see. All the warning signs are there. They tell us and show us what their intentions are, yet most people refuse to take them at their word. In this book I hope to stir people to take a look at what is coming and to get ready.

authorHOUSE®

AuthorHouse™
1663 Liberty Drive, Suite 200
Bloomington, IN 47403
www.authorhouse.com
Phone: 1-800-839-8640

AuthorHouse™ *UK Ltd.*
500 Avebury Boulevard
Central Milton Keynes, MK9 2BE
www.authorhouse.co.uk
Phone: 08001974150

First published by AuthorHouse 5/9/2007

ISBN: 978-1-4343-0600-5 (sc)

Library of Congress Control Number: 2007903488

Printed in the United States of America
Bloomington, Indiana

This book is printed on acid-free paper.

Dedicated to my family
My wife Caroline, and children; Timothy, Andrew, Larry &Cathy,
Stacie& Joe and all my wonderful and perfect grandbabies!

Contents

Introduction

The two Christ; which one will win?

In this book I will explain to you how Islam preaches another Jesus. They admit that He came to earth and preached and that He performed miracles. They do not admit that He died. Nor do they believe that He was raised from the dead and they refuse to accept that He is Immanuel, God with us. They will tell you that He was a great prophet, but He was not God. This is their doctrine and according to the Apostle Paul they are of the devil.

2Co 11:2-4 For I am jealous over you with godly jealousy: for I have espoused you to one husband that I may present you as a chaste virgin to Christ.

But I fear, lest by any means, as the serpent beguiled Eve through his subtlety, so your minds should be corrupted from the simplicity that is in Christ.

For if he that cometh preaches another Jesus, *whom we have not preached, or if ye receive another spirit, which ye have not received, or another gospel, which ye have not accepted.*

2Co 11:13-15 *For such ones are **false apostles**, deceitful workers, transforming themselves into the apostles of Christ.*

Did not even Satan marvelously transform himself into an angel of light? Therefore it is no great thing if his ministers also transform themselves as ministers of righteousness, whose end shall be according to their works.

Here the Apostle Paul speaks of someone preaching "another Jesus". The idea of another Jesus should be understood as meaning even someone who acknowledges with their mouths Jesus Christ, yet by their doctrines and beliefs denies Him.

In 1John 2:23 *John said that anyone who denies the Son has not the Father. In the Greek it says "hath not even the Father".* **So it is scripturally impossible for the Muslims to have God without accepting the Son.**

In the book of Revelation the conflict will be between the two Christ. One will lay claim to the name but will follow the teachings of Muhammad. The other one, the real one, will rule first from Heaven and finally on Earth. The Battle of Armageddon will be the culmination of this conflict; who actually is the Christ? Is it the Jesus of the Bible or the Muslim Jesus? There can be no doubt that the Jesus of God's Word is not the same one that is described as the false prophet in chapter 13 of the Book of Revelation.

Muslims say Jesus was a great prophet but nothing more. That is why the **second beast is called a prophet**; he will be their version of Jesus. He is the one who will do miracles in the presence of the antichrist. He will deny all essential Christian doctrines. There can only be one Jesus. The war will determine which one will reign.

This is the battle line that is drawn. Either Jesus is who He claimed to be or else He was a fraud. Ask yourself something, who would have the most to gain by saying that Jesus was a failure? The only logical answer is the devil. If he can convince man that Jesus was not who He claimed to be then the plan of salvation was for nothing and not just Jesus but God Himself was a failure. As you study the Bible from Genesis to Revelation you will see one solid thought permeating the book; there will come one who will redeem mankind. He is the one who will crush the serpents head. He will be the one called the Messiah. He will lead the people of God back to God. He is in every book of the Old Testament. We know Him as Jesus. He was before all things. He created all things. They were created thru Him, by Him and for Him. This book is a study of the book of Revelation. In it I seek to make clear some things that are clouded by preconceived thinking. I take the book as it is written. I believe in the inerrancy of scripture. The Word of God is pure. Please read it carefully and prayerfully. Ask the Holy Spirit to help in your study.

This book is the result of years of research and study of the Word of God. I don't think it is perfect, because I am not perfect. I do believe that it will help anyone who wants to understand the book of the Revelation. It is not intended to replace the study of the book; rather it is a study guide to help to better understand it. Read along in your Bible as you study the guide and learn the wonderful truths contained in the Book of the Revelation. In this study book I have skipped over much of the first four chapters of Revelation. I did this because so many have already written about those chapters. I wanted to focus on the more difficult to understand parts of the book.

God never intended for us to be ignorant of His Word.

Deut. 29:29; *The secret things belong unto Jehovah our God; but the things that are revealed belong unto us and to our children for ever, that we may do all the words of this law. It is my hope that I will help everyone to understand the book of Revelation, allowing them to get a quick understanding of the last book in the Bible. It is a simple gospel written for a simple people. I hope that I have presented it in a simple way. The Revelation above all New Testament books draws upon the Old Testament. In all over 250 times. So it is important to understand the Old as well as the New Testament if you are to understand what God is saying.*

I believe the secret to understanding the book of Revelation is really simple; it is a **religious book**, so read it as a **religious book**. Politics has nothing to do with this book. It will not be a battle of political parties. It will be a battle of religion. Religion is the cause and reason that it was written. Religion is the thought that runs thru the entirety of the story. Worship is Gods' alone but the devil has always wanted to be worshipped. That is the cause of his rebellion and the drive behind the antichrist-the desire to be worshipped. The world will worship the antichrist and thru him, satan. The church and heaven worship the Lamb and God. That is the line that is drawn. That is the cause of the war that follows. Religion is what decides everything in the Revelation. Which side will win? That is what the book is about.

Based on the latest data, it appears that in about 50 years there will only be two dominant religions on earth; Islam and Christianity. Only one can be right. Either Jesus is only a prophet or He is the Son of God. This book is intended to help you decide. Ask yourself this; what does God mean by the word Revelation? What is it about Jesus that He is revealing? The answer is His Divinity.

Chapter one

Rev. 1:1

<u>The Revelation of Jesus Christ, which God gave unto him,</u>

This is the Title that God gave to the book. Its purpose is the **Revealing of Jesus Christ**, whom Heaven must receive **until the Times of the Restitution of All things, <u>Acts 3:21.</u>** This then is the time for God to restore all things, whether in Heaven or on the Earth or beneath the Earth. Jesus <u>IS NOW LORD</u>, but He shall be shown to be Lord even to those who oppose Him. Of all the New Testament books, Revelation has the clearest purpose. It is to make clear to the entire universe that Jesus is the eternal Lord of Lords and King of Kings in heaven and earth and even under the earth. He is Lord over the living and the dead.

Notice the title; the Revealing of Jesus the Messiah **which God gave unto Him.** This continues the theme that John developed in the Gospel of John of the faithful servant. Over 40 times in the Gospel Jesus makes the statement **that He was sent, God was the one in charge.** Here God begins the process of conferring on Jesus <u>the promised Kingdom.</u>

"For He must reign until He shall have put down all enemies under His feet" <u>1 Cor. 15:25.</u>

*"Thou hast put all things in subjection under his feet. For in that he put all in subjection under him, he left nothing that is not put under him. **But now we see not yet all things put under him.** 9But we see Jesus, who was made a little lower than the angels for the suffering of death, crowned with glory and honor; that he by the grace of God should taste death for every man".* **<u>Hebrews 2:8-9</u>**

1

<u>Part one; the revealing of Jesus to His body the church, Revelation Chapters 1-3</u>

<u>**1:1**</u> *"**To show unto His servant's** things which must shortly come to pass; and he sent and signified it by his angel unto his servant John"*

God intended for us to **see** what He was **showing** us. He never intended for us to be ignorant of what was going to come to pass. So why are so many confused about the book? I believe it's because they don't read it **as it is,** but rather as **they think it is.** Rather than trying to fit the contents into our theology of the day, we should accept what God says.

One more reason many people can't make sense of the Book of the Revelation is because they insist on reading it from an America centered or European centered view. <u>Israel is the central theme of the book</u> once the rapture has taken place. <u>Jerusalem is the apple of Gods eye now and forever.</u>

We can't lose sight of this clear teaching from scripture. I believe all the contents of the book apply to the last days. Although there are some obvious things that applied in John's day, such as the warnings to the seven churches, <u>they have a double prophetic meaning.</u> Some prophecies obviously apply to two circumstances or people. For instance David wrote several Psalms that applied to him, yet also applied to Jesus Christ.

<u>***Rev. 1:11***</u> *"**Write on a scroll what you see, and send it to the seven churches:***

1. <u>*Ephesus,*</u>
2. <u>*Smyrna,*</u>
3. <u>*Pergamum,*</u>
4. <u>*Thyatira,*</u>
5. <u>*Sardis,*</u>
6. <u>*Philadelphia,*</u>
7. <u>*Laodicea."*</u>

Many prefer to view the seven churches as seven time periods of the one church. In the day that the book was written, all seven churches existed simultaneously. They obviously would have understood it for its immediate meaning. I believe that the same rule should apply to our time and all times. The message to the churches is relevant today for all churches worldwide. At the time of the rapture, all seven churches will be on earth. In fact, they exist right now. All you have to do is look for them.

All seven churches were within traveling distance of each other. Therefore it stands to reason that anything happening at one church was probably known to the others.

Some of the churches knew the apostle Paul and therefore would have known Timothy and Titus. Doctrinally they should have been pure. Paul mentions two by name- Laodocia and Ephesus. They are at polar opposites from each other spiritually.

First let us list the warnings and then we will list the promises.

1.   THE WARNINGS TO THE END TIME CHURCH;

"I have a few things against you."

Chapters two and three

1. You have left your first love; your love has grown cold. **2:4-5**
2. You allow the doctrine of Balaam, the doctrine of compromise, to be in your midst.**2:14**
3. You allow the doctrine of the Nicolaitans, the doctrine of false knowledge. The Nicolaitans allowed paganism and perversion to mix with Christianity **2:15**. According to ancient sources, Nicolas the originator of this sect was the same man who had been a deacon in the early church, **Acts 6:5.** He was then a man of reputation who compromised the purity of the truth and allowed the influences of the world and false wisdom to pollute the gospel.
4. You allow Jezebel to teach and seduce my servants. According to ancient sources, this woman was the pastor's wife. She was allowed to teach the church as one who was truly spiritual, yet her teaching caused the people to commit sin. **2:20.** Jezebel was the queen who destroyed true worship and placed her own false religion in its place. She demanded total control.
5. Repent, or else I will come as a thief and you will miss my coming. **3:3.** it is possible to miss the rapture.

6. <u>You are wretched, miserable, poor, blind and naked</u>. Return to the Lord and receive what you really need. **<u>3:17.</u>**

<u>THE PROMISES TO THE SEVEN CHURCHES:</u>

"To him who overcomes, I will give;

1. The crown of life
2. The tree of life
3. The hidden manna
4. A new name written on a white stone
5. Authority to rule the nations with Christ, (1,000 years).
6. A white robe
7. His name will be written in the book of life
8. <u>He will be kept from the tribulation</u>
9. He will be a pillar in Gods temple where he shall belong from now on
10. Three new names will be written on him
11. Authority to sit on the throne of Christ (rule under His authority)

Behold I stand at the door and knock. If any man will hear My voice and open the door I will come in and sup with him and he with Me. <u>Chapter 3:21</u>. The promise is still as fresh and meaningful today as it was 2,000 years ago. Jesus still knocks on the hearts door, will you answer His call? The promise to be kept from the hour of tribulation should be enough to make everyone want to be ready. All of these promises are only for those who overcome. They also are only for those who follow Jesus. How do we overcome? By the word of our testimony and the Blood of the Lamb.

The characteristics of the seven churches can definitely be found today around the world. **Ephesus,** the loving church is still alive and well. **Smyrna,** the church that dwells where satan lives is still alive in places like <u>Iran, North Korea, China, Las Vegas and San Francisco</u>. **Pergamos,** the compromising church is in the news everyday. They are the ones voting to allow gay marriage and are taking the blood out of their hymnbooks.

Thyatira, the sinful church that allows sin to flourish is still peddling its product. **Sardis,** the weak church is still hobbling along, barely able to keep going. **Philadelphia,** the on-fire church that is uncompromising in its stand is still preaching the truth. **Laodicea,** the self absorbed dead church that has everything it desires is still on television. Laodicea is much more concerned about what the world thinks of them than what Jesus thinks.

In fact, Laodicea appeals more to the world than it does to God. Popularity and prestige are what sets the Laodician church apart from the rest. Its wealth and prosperity were its hallmark. Laodicea was lukewarm, neither hot nor cold. The sad thing about them was that they didn't know the state they were in. Jesus advised them to buy from Him gold tried in the fire and white raiment to cover their nakedness and salve for their eyes. They are in a wretched state of life and do not realize it.

The warnings and promises of Jesus are still applicable to us today. They are meant for all time to every church in all circumstances. To limit them to a specific time is to limit them altogether. Jesus presents to us wonderful promises if we will just take them from His hands.

Rev. 1:12-16

And I turned to see the voice that spoke with me. And being turned, ***I saw seven golden candlesticks;*** *13 And in the **midst of the seven candlesticks** one like unto the <u>Son of man,</u> clothed with a garment down to the foot, and girt about the paps with a golden girdle. <u>**14**His head and his hairs</u> were **<u>white like wool</u>**, as white as snow; and his **<u>eyes were as a flame of fire</u>**; 15 And his feet like unto fine brass, as if they burned in a furnace; and his voice as the sound of many waters. **16 And he had in his right hand seven stars:** and out of his mouth went a sharp two-edged sword: and his countenance was as the sun shines in his strength.*

Here Jesus is pictured standing in the middle of His churches. Much like a good gardener will inspect his garden the Lord inspects His. He is sending a message to the churches, "**<u>you belong to Me</u>**". The majesty of Jesus is what John saw. He looked like God for a reason, because He is Immanuel, God with us.

He had in His right hand- **the hand of power**- the seven stars. This also signifies His ownership.

Rev. 1:17-20
*And when I saw Him, I fell at His feet as dead. But He laid His right hand on me, saying to me, "Do not be afraid; I am the First and the Last. 18I am He who lives, and was dead, and behold, I am alive forevermore. Amen. And I have the keys of Hades and of Death. 19Write the things **which you have seen**; and the **things which are**; and the **things which will take place** after this. 20The mystery of the seven stars which you saw in My right hand, and the seven golden lamp stands: the seven stars are the **angels of the seven churches**, and **the seven lamp stands** which you saw **are the seven churches**.*

The keys are important because of what they represent. In the Greek the word translated "key" means "the ability to shut or open". What Jesus is saying here is that He alone has the ability to close up the power of the grave or death, not the devil or anyone else.

The seven angels; literally means the seven messengers. This is to say that they are the local leaders of the churches-the pastors. The fact that He has them in His hands does not imply that He is always pleased with the pastor. It does imply that no matter what Jesus is in control of their lives. Whether they do good or bad, He will not relinquish His control. There is a warning accompanying this; punishment and reward come from the same source. So whether it is the leader or a layman in the church, we will all answer to Him and Him alone. As a husbandman is responsible for the outcome of the crop, Jesus takes His responsibility seriously. Even the Laodocian church is His. This also means that He alone has the right to inspect and find fault.

Romans 14:4 *Who are you to judge another's servant? To his own master he stands or falls. Indeed, he will be made to stand, for God is able to make him stand.*

We are His and He is ours. Whatever claim the world, the devil or man may make on us, that claim is destroyed thru Christ. He is our master. He paid full price to get us!

1 Cor. 6:20 *For you were bought with a price; therefore glorify God in your body and in your spirit, which are God's.*

1 Cor. 7:23
__You were bought with a price__; do not become slaves of men.

Jesus deals with the church first.

Judgment must begin with the church before the tribulation period. Jesus spoke to the churches first. Then He dealt with the Heavens, then the earth. The church is going to go thru a period of SIFTING, SORTING and PURIFYING before the rapture. Right now the church of the Lord Jesus Christ is entering into a new stage; a time where the Lord is weeding out and putting a new heart into His church.

In America and around the world there is a cry for the true power of God to be shown. God is causing His people to grow weary of the fake and the sideshows. They know God is real and want to see His power in their lives. At the same time there are many who prefer to keep going on as if everything is fine. They cannot hear the voice of God calling to them. Before Jesus came the first time the spirit of Elijah was sent before Him in the person of John the Baptist. Before He comes the second time Jesus said Elijah himself would come. But what about the rapture generation? If the spirit of Elijah came the first time, and Elijah will come the second time, wouldn't that same anointing be sent before the rapture? I believe it will.

What is the spirit of Elijah? **Luke 1:17** says he will turn the hearts of the people. So there has to be a heart changing coming for those who are listening to God. The Elijah anointing is coming on the church. Jesus will thoroughly purge His floor, Matthew 3:10 & **Luke 3:17.** So before we get too busy thinking about what is going to happen to the world, we had better get ready for what Jesus is going to do to us.

Part two; the revealing of Jesus to Heaven

Revelation chapter four, the heavens are opened to John.

I know it will mess up some people's theology, but there is no reason to say that the rapture takes place in chapter four. When Jesus calls John to "**come up here**" it is directed **at John**. Otherwise we will all be told "**things that shall be hereafter**". The reason for John to come up was to allow **HIM** to see what was going to happen so that **HE** could tell us.

John was caught up to heaven, "in the spirit". He was not translated as the bible says we will be at the rapture **(1 Thessalonians 4:13-17, 1 Corinthians 15:51-52).** Nor was he caught up in the clouds. He was taken by the Spirit to see things that would shortly come to pass. There was no trumpet blast, he was not raptured.

The throne is the focus of John's attention. He sees the One upon the throne in all His beauty and splendor. Power is evident, lightning flashes and thunder rolls. Twenty-four elders are representative of all redeemed mankind; twelve from the Old Testament, and twelve from the New. They are wearing crowns of gold and are clothed in white raiment and are around the throne. Next John describes the Seraphim that Ezekiel also saw. Chapter four ends with a song of praise to the Lord.

Revelation chapter five; the taking of the book by Jesus

John sees a book written inside and out in the right hand of God who was sitting on the throne. The right hand is significant because it denotes power and authority **(Exodus 15:6, 15:12, Isaiah 41:10, 48:13, Hebrews 1:3).** The call was made for one who was worthy to open the book. The word translated as worthy actually means "deserving". The same word is found in **Hebrews 3:3;** *for He was counted **worthy** of more glory than Moses, because he who has built the house has more honor than the house.*

All of Heaven and Earth were unworthy and undeserving to take the book from Gods right hand. Only one who had proved Himself as deserving could even consider taking it. This was more than a test of strength or of character. To be able to take the book meant that He had conquered the enemy of God in open warfare. No angel or man could make this claim except Jesus.

The Lion of the tribe of Judah has prevailed to open the book. Yet instead of seeing a Lion, John sees a Lamb, slain yet alive. **1Peter 1:18-20** *knowing that you were not redeemed with corruptible things, silver or gold, from your vain manner of life handed down from your fathers, **but with the precious blood of Christ, as of a lamb without blemish and without spot;** indeed having been foreknown before the foundation of the world, but revealed in the last times for you,*

What happened from the Cross to the Throne?

The Bible tells us much about the three days that Jesus was dead. He was dead to man, but He was very active in the spirit. He went to the heart of the earth and conquered death and the grave and in the process He also conquered the devil, **Hebrews 2:14.** It is important to understand Jewish beliefs at the time that Jesus lived. When He spoke of the rich man and Lazarus, in **Luke 16:19-31,** He was talking about something that all Jews except the Sadducees believed. According to Jesus there were two compartments in the heart of the earth. One was called hell and the other was called paradise or Abraham's bosom.

Hell is a place I don't think needs too much explanation. It is a place of intense heat and torment where all unrighteous go.

The place that is called Abrahams bosom was also called Paradise by Jesus when he was talking with the thief on the cross in **Luke 23:43.** All righteous people who had ever died were there. From Abel to the thief on the cross, every one of them was there. It was a place of peace and joy, but it was not heaven.

So what exactly does the Bible say happened? Let's start at the end, where really it all began. Jesus drew His last breath and cried out, *"It is finished!"* and let out a loud cry and said, *"Father into Your hands I commend My Spirit"* and died. Immediately the veil in the temple was torn from top to bottom and the earth quaked, **Matthew 27:51.**

Then according to **1Peter 3:18-20** He went to preach to the sinners in hell. The word translated as "preached" is the word "kerusso" in the Greek. It does not actually mean to preach, but to proclaim, as in, the

9

judge proclaimed the verdict. Peter tells us that these were unrighteous people. There is no doubt that the message that Jesus gave them was one of judgment. The tenor of the original Greek is not what we would find in the preaching of deliverance or of salvation.

We are told in **John 19:31-32** that the two thieves had their legs broken by the Roman soldiers. This prevented them from being able to push their selves up so that they could breath. This forced them to suffocate quickly on the cross. One thief repented to the Lord and one did not. Jesus told the repentant thief that he would be with the Him that day in Paradise. The other one went straight to hell. While Jesus was proclaiming the judgment of the sinners in hell, the unrepentant thief fell into the flames.

Next we are told in **1Peter 4:5-6** that Jesus went to preach the Gospel to those who were dead. Gospel means "good news". Jesus arrived in Paradise with the good news of His conquest over the devil. **1 John 3:8**, *for this purpose was the Son of God manifested, so that He might destroy the works of the devil.* Every saint who had ever died was told the good news. There no doubt was great joy and rejoicing.

In **Psalms 68:18** and **Ephesians 4:8** we are told that He led captivity captive. What this means is that Jesus set the captives in Paradise free. **Matthew 27:52** says that after His resurrection many of the dead saints were seen for a short while in Jerusalem. They were not in physical bodies but were in spiritual form. What happened was this; Jesus led the saints free from their place of containment. As He led them up to heaven, He stopped and talked with Mary Magdalene in **John 20:14-17.** The phrase "touch me not" in verse 17 should read "don't detain Me". He could be touched, but not detained. **John 20:17;** *Jesus saith to her, Touch me not; **for I am not yet ascended unto the Father: but go unto my brethren, and say to them, I ascend unto my Father and your Father, and my God and your God.***

When He ascended, He led captivity captive. Yet He stopped to comfort Mary. That was when the sainted dead appeared to many. And the reason why it was only that one time was that Jesus continued on His journey to see the Father. Jesus is Lord over death, hell and the grave. He triumphed over them all.

The greatest passage on Jesus appearing before the Father is in **Daniel 7 :13** I *saw in the night-visions, and, behold, there came with* *the clouds of heaven one like unto a **son of man**, and he came even to the ancient of days, and they brought him near before him.* **Dan 7:14** *And there was given him dominion, and glory, and a kingdom, that all the peoples, nations, and languages should serve him: his dominion is an everlasting dominion, which shall not pass away, and his kingdom that which shall not be destroyed.*

We see that the whole host of heaven assembled to usher Jesus into the presence of the Father. The Father gave Him His kingdom and glory. This was the coronation of the King of Kings and the Lord of Lords. What a wonderful sight it was to see.

Heb 2:10 *For it became him, for whom are all things, and **through** whom are all things, in bringing many sons unto glory, to make the author of their salvation perfect through sufferings.*

Heb 2:11 *For both he that sanctifieth and they that are sanctified are all of one: for which cause he is not ashamed to call them brethren,*

Heb 2:12 *saying, I will declare thy name unto my brethren, In the midst of the congregation will I sing thy praise.*

Heb 2:13 *and again, I will put my trust in him. And again behold, I and the children whom God hath given me.*

Jesus introduced His brethren, newly adopted into the New Covenant by His blood. They in turn proclaimed His worth and majesty to all of Heaven as the one who conquered the enemy. **Verse 13** then proclaims Gods' ownership of the children. This is what happened after Jesus died. It was not a time of quietness in the spirit world. In fact, as far as the devil and his forces were concerned, it was the worst three days they had ever had!

It is Muslim doctrine that God can't have a son, so therefore Jesus could not be Gods' son. **"Far be it from His [Allah's] glory that He should have a son!"— The Koran, Sura IV.** This quote is from Muhammad. It is central to their doctrine that God is not Jesus' Father.

The belief in God being called **Father** originated **with God**. In the very first book in the Bible, **Genesis 6:2&4** God called angels the "sons of God". In what is perhaps the oldest book in the Bible, the book of **Job, chapters 1:6, 2:1 and 38:7** all proclaim Angels to be the "sons of God".

God told David that He Himself would be a **Father** to Solomon, **1Chronicles 28:6.** In **Psalm 2:7** God declared that He would be a **Father** to the Messiah.

Hosea 1:10 *Yet the number of the children of Israel shall be as the sand of the sea, which cannot be measured nor numbered; and it shall come to pass that, in the place where it was said unto them, Ye are not my people,* <u>*it shall be said unto them, Ye are the sons of the living God.*</u> Obviously it was always Gods intent to be a **Father** to mankind. This was and always has been scripturally sound teaching.

The Jews never denied that God could have a son; what they denied was that Jesus was that son. Only in Islam do we find this kind of teaching against a well established Bible teaching. Regardless of what they say, **Jesus is Gods Son**. End of the debate. Jesus claimed He was, God claimed He was, and all of His disciples claimed He was. **1John 2:22** *Who is a liar but he who denies that Jesus is the Christ?* <u>*He who denies the Father and the Son is antichrist.*</u>

1John 2:23 <u>*Everyone who denies the Son neither has the Father.*</u> *The one confessing the Son also has the Father.*

Was Jesus God?

1Ti 3:16 *And without controversy great is the mystery of godliness:* <u>***God was manifested in the flesh,***</u> *justified in the Spirit, seen by angels, preached among nations, believed on in the world, and received up into glory.* There is no doubt that Paul is talking about Jesus. God was manifested in the flesh. **Psalms 45:6** *Your throne, O God, is forever and ever; the staff of Your kingdom is a staff of righteousness.* In the book of Hebrews the writer quotes this verse as applying to Jesus. When Jesus resurrected and appeared to Thomas, Thomas called Him "my Lord and My God". Jesus did not correct him or stop him from worshipping Him. He said He was the "I AM". That is the name of God Jehovah. Israel understood what He meant.

It is clear from many other scriptures that the disciples who were with Jesus for 3.5 years accepted Him as God in the flesh-Immanuel as prophesied by Isaiah. There really was no doubt in the early church until long after the original apostles had died. Only then could the devil make people believe that Jesus was just a man. Read also Johns' Gospel. He is God.

Man was made in the exact image of God, Genesis **1:27.** In **1Thess. 5:23** we are told that man has a "spirit", "soul" and "body".

Since man was made in Gods exact image, and man has a spirit, soul and body, then it makes sense that God also would have a Spirit, Soul and Body.

The Spirit of God is the Holy Spirit. He is a person according to Jesus in **John 14:16**. He can be grieved according to **Ephesians 4:30.** The Spirit of God is God.

The Soul is "psuche" in the Greek. It means the mind and the emotions. Does God have emotions? Yes He does. He told Moses that He could become angry, grieved, and jealous and that He could love. The fruit of the Spirit in **Galations 5:22-23** *"But the fruit of the Spirit is: love, joy, peace, long-suffering, kindness, goodness, faith, meekness, self-control; against such things there is no law"* are emotional descriptions. You can not love or have joy without involving emotions. Clearly then God has emotions. What about the mind? Does God have a central mind? Consider this fact; over 40 times in the Gospel of John Jesus said that He did not come on His own. He said the Father sent Him, told Him what to do and what to say. He said it was the Fathers will that He was doing not His own. There is another word for will that means the same thing; mind. The Father is the mind.

So then that leaves us looking for the Body of God. Does God have a body? Hebrews says that He does. **Heb 10:5-10** *Therefore when He comes into the world, He says, "Sacrifice and offering You did not desire,* ***but You have prepared a body for Me****.*
In burnt offerings and sacrifices for sin You have had no pleasure.
Then I said, Lo, I come (in the volume of the Book it is written of Me) ***to do Your will, O God."***
Above, when He said, "Sacrifice and offering, and burnt offerings and offering for sin You did not desire, neither did You have pleasure in them" (which are offered according to the Law),
then He said, "Lo, I come to do Your will, O God." He takes away the first so that He may establish the second.
By this will we are sanctified through the offering of ***the body*** *of Jesus Christ once for all.*

Jesus is the body of God. He is God manifest in the Flesh. So there you have God- Spirit, Soul, and Body. The triune God. And all the fullness dwelt bodily in Christ.

Many scholars have speculated on why John wept. I believe John wept because he personally knew Jesus was worthy, yet he did not see Jesus come forward or heaven acknowledge Him right away. If you knew Jesus like John did you would have expected Jesus to immediately receive the acknowledgment He deserved.

The reason for the delay in the recognition of Christ may have to do with the fact that He had to fight to get what was His. It was not easy for Him, yet He overcame.

What God is doing in chapter five is reinforcing the divinity of His Son, Jesus Christ. Only the spotless Lamb can take the book out of God's hand. Only the divine can claim what is obviously a divine right, the ownership of the book. This then is a picture of what John said in the title; the Revelation of Jesus Christ, which God gave unto Him.

For those who refuse to acknowledge that Jesus and the Father are different and separate I ask, how did Jesus give Himself the book? Jesus is described as the Lion yet appears as the Lamb. While on earth He was indeed a lamb, **Isaiah 53:7,** yet from this point on He takes on the characteristics of the Lion. Just as a lion will defend his own and protect his territory, even so does Jesus begin to exert His authority on this earth.

The Revelation then is seen as a progressive process. Jesus reveals His majesty in steps to the world. The book is best understood in this context. It is the act of revealing Jesus. The religion of the Church is dealt with first, then the religion of heaven. And next the religion of the earth will be dealt with. The devil demands worship. The antichrist will demand and receive worship. But only God and His Son **deserve worship**. The rest of the book deals with worship, who is really worthy and who will receive worship. By the end of this book I seek to prove the divinity of Jesus Christ, the Son of God.

Chapter two

The opening of the seven seals and what they mean

Birthpangs: The Beginning Of The End

MATTHEW 24:8 & Mark 13:8 &1 Thess.5:3
All these are the beginning of sorrows (birth pangs)

To get the full meaning of the book of Revelation, we need to take the entire Bible into account. No one book is intended to stand alone. The entirety of the Bible is drawn upon as a resource work in Revelation. To get the meaning of the pictures and types you must **understand where they are drawn from.** Only that way will you get what God is saying to us. All works of God support and do not contradict one another.

For instance, many scholars point to chapter four of Revelation as the point where the rapture takes place. **Why do they say this?** They can't reconcile the Words of Jesus in the Gospels where He talks about the rapture to anything in Revelation.

It's not that His words don't reconcile, it's that they would mean <u>we have to face adversity before the rapture of the church.</u> **If you take the signs that Jesus talks about and line them up to the sixth chapter of Revelation, you have a perfect match.** The problem with this is that it makes it appear to some that the antichrist is loosed on the earth before the rapture. If we look to scripture we will find that according to <u>**1 John 3:18**</u> there already were in his day "many antichrists". The **spirit of antichrist** is already loosed on this earth.

The **person of antichrist** is not yet loosed. To understand the spirit of antichrist you need only look at Muhammad or Hitler. They both had an intense hatred of anyone who disagreed with them. They both especially hated the Jews. Both tried to kill as many Jews as possible.

Both were precursors to the real antichrist, the one who will personify their hatred.

But who is this man? Can he be alive right now? I think a little common sense will help us here. The antichrist is a living breathing man. He will not suddenly materialize out of thin air. Therefore he has to be full grown and mature before the rapture. He is alive before we leave! Think about it. Maybe we have all seen him on the news already. Or perhaps he hasn't exposed himself yet. Either way, he can be <u>alive and hindered</u> at the same time. One thing is clear from scripture; <u>he can't take over until he is allowed to</u>. God holds the reigns.

The birth pangs have begun!

CONCERNING THE SEALS; think of the seals like a snowball. As it starts downhill it gets larger and larger, until it becomes an avalanche. The things that are represented by the seals start out small then grow gradually larger and fiercer. They will build in intensity as the tribulation progresses until they reach a thundering crescendo at the battle of Armageddon. **These are the birth pangs; they have already started and are growing in intensity even now.**

Matthew speaks of birth pangs in <u>verse 8</u>. Just as in childbirth a woman's pains start out mild and far apart, and then increase in severity and get harder and closer together, so will it be in the end.

The first five seals are already opened; the sixth is the next one. You only have to study a little history to see that the things described in chapter six have already been loosed on the world. From false prophets to persecution of the church, they had already started by the first century.

In the beginning of the sorrows, the birth pangs were hard to diagnose. For some there is still a denial that they have even started. Yet to those watching, it can't be denied. <u>The beginning of the end has definitely started.</u>

I believe that they started in 1967. That was when Israel took the city of Jerusalem back after almost 2,000 years of Gentile occupation. From that moment, the rise of radical Islam has increased in its severity. Like a dam break, they are surging out in an attempt to conquer the world.

A quick check of terrorist attacks will show that since 1967 the attacks have gotten more frequent with each passing year. The goal of these people is to not only destroy our nation, but to force all people to adopt Islam or die.

There are two views of Jesus in the world today. One says that He was a good man, probably even a great man, but He was not the Son of God. **The other view is the one the Bible puts forth, namely that Jesus is God in the flesh, that He died and rose again and that He is the Son of God.** The final conflict is between these opposing views. Only one of them can be victorious. Religion will be the fuel to the devils fire.

I believe that the religion of Islam is the religion of antichrist. As I will show, it is against all of the core Christian doctrines defined in the Bible. Please understand I don't hate or condemn the people of Islam. I do however show how deluded men can be when they will not question their beliefs.

Definitons; The Mahdi, the Dajjil, and the false Jesus

I want to give some definitions of some of the characters who figure in the end time's prophecies. I will quote from Islamic sources and of course from the Bible. **When I use the Islamic sources please understand that that does not mean that I put faith in them.** The reason I use them is to show that the devil is setting the stage for the antichrist. The only way anyone can garner a worldwide following is if they tie it to a **religious theme.** That is how the antichrist will rise to power, religion.

The man we will call antichrist is the one the Muslims call the **Mahdi.**

The **Dajjil** is the Muslim term for the prophet who will be in Jerusalem; they call him "antichrist". We believe this to be Enoch and Elijah. **Hebrews 9:27,** *"it is appointed to men once to die and after this the Judgment"*. Neither Enoch nor Elijah has died yet. The Muslims believe and teach that Jesus will come to earth again to convert the world to Islam. The **false prophet** who assists the antichrist is the person that the Muslims will call Jesus. He will be a false Christ.

For every truth, the devil has a lie. It is no different today in Islam, the person **they claim** to be the antichrist is in reality the one who is sent from God. They refuse to accept his preaching because the devil has deluded them. Not only has the devil deceived them, but according to **2 Thessalonians 2:11**, God shall send on them a strong delusion so that they may continue to believe the lie.

The devil knows that he has but a short time left that is why he is working overtime to spread his lies about Jesus. The spirit of compromise is still alive in the church today.

The Mahdi

The Mahdi means the "guided one". He is said to be in "Occultation", which means hidden by God. The place where most believe that he is at is in a deep cave or well in the city of Samarra, Iraq. There is a mosque built over the well and many pilgrims go there to pray to him every year.

This is very important to understanding the wars among Muslims; the Shiites believe it was the Sunnis who drove the Mahdi to hide. They also believe that he will lead the "true Muslims" against the false ones in a series of great wars.

There are several Muslim prophecies concerning him.

They state that; he will be named after his alleged ancestor Muhammad. He will be about 40 at the time of his appearing. He will rule the world for seven years. The world will be in a state of chaos before he comes. He will fight many battles against other Muslims. He will make a seven years peace treaty with several nations of the world including Israel. He will eventually seek to destroy Israel and every Jew on planet earth.

Also of note is this prophecy; after about three years of horrendous world chaos, he along with Jesus would lead the Muslims to conquer the unbelievers and their leader in Jerusalem.

As you can see the devil is preparing the way for this man to take over. Islam is longing for the Mahdi. He is said to act exactly like Muhammad. That is a frightening thought!

The false prophet; the one claiming to be Jesus

Contrary to what you may have heard, Muslims believe in Jesus. They don't believe in the Biblical version of Jesus though. Their version is very different. Here is some of what they believe he will be.

They believe he will appear near or in Damascus at a time when the Mahdi will be gathering his armies to battle the Jews and their prophets in Jerusalem. Their Jesus will be a follower of Islam and subject himself to the Mahdi. He will not even dare to pray in the Mahdis presence. According to Muhammad, Jesus was just a prophet, nothing more. Therefore this Jesus will only claim to be a prophet.

According to the Islamic prophecies he will lead the Mahdis armies against the Jews and retake the temple mount. He will kill many people himself. He will deflect all glory to the Mahdi. In fact he will seek no reward or recognition for himself but will seek to exalt the Mahdi.

The false Jesus will purify the Muslims and turn them back to "correct Islam" or "pure Islam". All who do not follow the Mahdi will be destroyed by this Jesus.

He will be able to do many miracles to prove he is Jesus. He will not have any visible scars from the crucifixion because he was never crucified, according to Muhammad. He will personally kill many people.

As you can see for yourself, Islam is expecting and waiting for these men to come. Christians are too. Except that we call them the antichrist and false prophet.

Here is the Muslim view of Jesus and the end-time; "Jesus Christ (whom the Moslems call Hadhrat Isa, the Messiah of Guidance) also figures prominently in Muslim prophecy. Christians deny the validity of the prophet Mohammed but his followers acknowledge Jesus Christ as a great prophet, albeit not as the **demigod that Christians** have made of him. In the opinion of Moslems, Jesus was sent only to the Children of Israel. **He had no responsibility whatsoever to other nations or people**."

In other words, they only accept part of Jesus, not all of Him. For us He is either God incarnate or He is a liar. They would have Him being born of a virgin, but not Divine. He can't possibly be one without being the other. We know Him as Immanuel, God with us!

Here is another quote; The Surah an-Nisaaa (4:156-159) condemns the Jews for their killing of Jesus and states that <u>Allah declares their claims to be false.</u> According to Moslem doctrine, a disciple who resembled Jesus sacrificed himself voluntarily: "And because of their **(the Jews)** saying, 'We killed Messiah, Jesus son of Mary, the Messenger of Allah' --- **but they killed him not, nor crucified him, but it was made to appear to them so. (This is the teaching that Judas or one of the other disciples died in Jesus' place. A preposterous notion to say the least.)** "But Allah raised him up (with his body and soul) unto Himself; and Allah is Ever All-Powerful, All-Wise".

For the Muslim, there is not a chance that they will believe anything except what Muhammad has said. It is forbidden for them to question Muhammad or Allah, so they can't even question the many contradictions in the Koran for fear of incurring damnation. How much harder it will be to get them to listen to the Bible.

Muslims insist that the Christians and Jews changed Gods' word. Here are a couple of Muhammad's sayings. "But the transgressors changed the word from that which had been given them" (2:59 AYA) they change words from their context and forget a part of that whereof they were admonished" (5:13 MP/14 AYA). **Muhammad told them that to even question him was the same as questioning God, so how can a Christian convince them that this isn't true?**

Quoting from the Koran I want to show you the religious basis for their actions. As you will see the Muslim can not even question the Koran.

Koran 48:13, <u>if any believes not in Allah and his messenger we have prepared a blazing fire for them.</u>

Koran 47:33, <u>believers obey Allah and obey the messenger. Do not falter, become faint hearted, or weak kneed, crying for peace.</u>

Ishaq 322 <u>Allah said, do not turn away from Muhammad when he is speaking to you. Do not contradict his orders.</u>

The fear of hell is enough to keep the Muslims in line. If one even acknowledges that there are contradictions in the Koran he is in danger of hell. According to the Bible, God made hell for the devil and his angels. According to Muhammad, demons, called jinn in Arabic, could get saved. **According to the Koran, even demons can believe**

in Islam. Koran 72:13 "so since we (jinn/demons) have listened to the guidance of the Koran we have accepted Islam.

According to Muhammad, Jesus never wanted to be worshipped, contrary to all that the New Testament says. And behold! God will say 'Oh Jesus, the son of Mary! Did you say unto men, worship me and my mother as gods in derogation of God?' He will say: 'Glory to Thee! Never could I say what I had no right (to say). Had I said such a thing, You would indeed have known it. You know what is in my heart, though I know not what is in Yours. "(5:116-117). Koran

You see how Jesus is shown to be less than what the Bible declares Him to be. Islam is violently anti-scripture and anti-Christ. They clearly do not worship the same God as Christians and Jews. Furthermore, Jesus never told anyone to worship Mary. That was a Catholic teaching which came much later.

Islam conquered much of Europe, the Middle East and Africa in the 8th century. Islam teaches that any land that was once Muslim must be re-conquered for Allah. They have designs on taking Europe back for Islam.

The first five seals are opened already and the spirits behind them are on the loose. They have not been able to take over because it is not time yet. When God allows them to, they will quickly assert control over the areas that God has given them to control.

Concerning the four horsemen and the four seals; the antichrist Mahdi (the white horse) will be the political head of the New Islamic Empire. The false Jesus (the false prophet) will cause the people to join the new religious order or die. The red horse signifies the coming religious war that will consume much of the world. The black horse signifies a new economy based on oil revenue. This will be controlled by the antichrist Mahdi. The pale horse signifies the sicknesses and disease that will spread rapidly across the globe during the tribulation.

What were the signs Jesus said to look for before the rapture?

1. ***False Christ and false prophets.* Matthew 24:5, Mark 13:6, Luke 21:8**
2. ***Wars and rumors of wars.* Mat.24:6, Mark13:7, Luke 21:9**

3. *Nation against nation literally means ethnic against ethnic.* **Mat. 24:7, Mark 13:8, Luke 21:10**
4. *Famines.* **Mat. 24:7, Mark 13:8, Luke 21:11**
5. *Earthquakes.* **Mat. 24:7, Mark 13:8, Luke 21:11**
6. *Pestilences.* **Mat. 24:7, Mark 13:8, Luke 21:11**
7. *Persecution for the cause of Christ.* **Mat. 24:9, Mark 13:9, Luke 21:12**
8. *Growing apathy and coldness of the Christians as the love of many would grow cold.* **Mat. 24:12, Mark 13:12, Luke 21:16**

Where do we see parallel scripture passages in the Bible? **In Revelation chapter six there is a parallel passage that says the same things.**

Notes on the scroll; it was rolled up with seven seals, which were usually wax. The contents of the book are not known simply by the breaking of the seals. The book has to be opened. The Revelation is inside the book and on its cover, but it has to be opened to get it. To teach that breaking the seals is something that happens after the rapture is not backed up by scripture. It is just that many do not take the time to study it out. These things have already started but are going to increase in severity.

The opening of the book is the revealing of Jesus, in other words, it contains His revelation.

Chapter three

The first seal; false Christ and false prophets, false religious teachers

Rev. 6:1-2 –Mat.24:5, Mk.13:6, Lk.21:8

I watched as the lamb opened the first of the seven seals. I heard one of the four living creatures say with a voice like thunder, "Go!" ²*Then I looked, and **there was a white horse, and its rider had a bow**. He was given a crown and rode off as a warrior to win battles.*

The riders appear to John as spirits, and we should understand them as such. It is obvious that there will be a man antichrist, yet it is also clear that there is a spirit behind him and that this spirit precedes him. All of these riders are spiritual. They directly affect the material world, and are later on personified by actual men, but they should be seen for the spiritual being they really are.

The birth pangs start out slow and then gather momentum. This is the way that the seals should be viewed. The spirits are released to do their work, yet it will take time for them to accomplish their work. It will start slow; yet will build in intensity until the pressure is so great that men's hearts will fail them for fear.

As bad as things may be on the earth right now, they are about to get a whole lot worse, and they will continue getting worse. They will continue to increase in intensity until they become almost overwhelming.

The leading horse is white; in Islam the teaching is that the Muslim mahdi, their deliverer, will come riding on a white horse. According to **Daniel 8:25**, the Antichrist will destroy many thru **PEACE**. For years bible teachers have taught that the coming antichrist was going to be a false Jesus. I believe that he will instead be a Muslim who will not claim to be Jesus at all, but will claim to be the promised deliverer of the world.

The Islamic teaching says that this is Muhammad riding the white horse in **Rev. 6:1**. While I definitely do not agree with that, I do believe that the spirit of antichrist found a suitable host in Muhammad. He embodied all the hate and religious fervor that the future antichrist will be known for, as well as a fanatical following that will gladly die for his cause.

It is also interesting to note another teaching from the Shiites; they teach that the mahdi will have all religions in his heart. In other words, he will relate to all false teachings and many of them will relate to him. Nearly every religion on earth teaches of a coming one who will usher in a new age. The Mahdi will give them what they want.

Many Muslim leaders such as Saddam Hussein have kept a white horse handy. No doubt they think that they might be the Mahdi. When he comes, he will speak great words against the true God. Daniel saw that he was given a mouth to speak against the saints of God.

OLD TESTAMENT DESCRIPTIONS OF THE ANTICHRIST

Ezekiel 28:1-5

The word of the LORD came to me again, saying,
2"Son of man, say to the prince of Tyre, 'Thus says the Lord GOD:
"Because your heart is lifted up, and you say, 'I am a god,
I sit in the seat of gods, (the rebuilt Holy of Holies)
In the midst of the seas,' (the midst of the seas refers to Jerusalem)
Yet you are a man, and not a god,
Though you set your heart as the heart of a god
3Behold, you are wiser than Daniel! (This refers to his satanic ability to speak great and hidden things that will amaze people)
There is no secret that can be hidden from you! (He is supernaturally
wise because the devil will tell him what to say.)
4With your wisdom and your understanding
You have gained riches for yourself,
And gathered gold and silver into your treasuries;
5By your great wisdom in trade (his financial dealings will prove
to be very prosperous for his followers too. They will receive of the

wealth as a way to buy their allegiance.)*You have increased your riches,*
And your heart is lifted up because of your riches," (Power corrupts and total power corrupts totally).

⁶ 'Therefore thus says the Lord God: "Because you have set your heart as the heart of a god, (He will really believe the devils lies, that he is a god)

⁷ Behold, therefore, I will bring strangers against you, The most terrible of the nations; And they shall draw their swords against the beauty of your wisdom, And defile your splendor. (The redeemed are literally from every nation and people. These are the ones who will return to fight along side Jesus at the battle of Armageddon).

⁸ They shall __*throw you down into the Pit,*__ *and you shall die the death of the slain In the midst of the seas.* (The beast will be taken at the battle of Armageddon and shall be cast into hell).

⁹ "Will you still say before him who slays you, 'I am a god'? *But you shall be a man, and not a god, in the hand of him who slays you.*

¹⁰ you shall die the death of the uncircumcised by the hand of aliens; for I have spoken," says the Lord God.' "

In the following passages God repeatedly refers to the antichrist as the Assyrian and the king of Babylon telling us where he will come from originally.

Isaiah 14:4-26 (NKJV)

⁴ (NKJV) that you will take up this proverb against the **king of Babylon,** *and say: "How the oppressor has ceased, the golden city ceased!*

⁵ The Lord has broken the staff of the wicked, the scepter of the rulers;

⁶ He who struck the people in wrath with a continual stroke, He who ruled the nations in anger, is persecuted and no one hinders. (This is a fitting picture of how the antichrist will rule and it is a result of hate. though he will come to power thru peace, it will be his hate that he will be known for).

⁷ The whole earth is at rest and quiet; they break forth into singing.

⁹ "Hell from beneath is excited about you, *to meet you at your coming; It stirs up the dead for you, All the chief ones of the earth; It has raised up from their thrones All the kings of the nations.*

(Again the Lord lets us know the destination of the antichrist is hell).

¹⁰ They all shall speak and say to you: 'Have you also become as weak as we? Have you become like us? (**Notice here that in hell people know one another, but there is no love**).

¹¹ Your pomp is brought down to Sheol, And the sound of your stringed instruments; <u>the maggot is spread under you, and worms cover you.</u>' (Hell is what God is speaking of here, a place that Jesus said their worm, that is maggot, dies not).

¹² "How you are fallen from heaven, O Lucifer, son of the morning! How you are cut down to the ground, you who weakened the nations! (**This prophecy has a double meaning in that it applies to both the devil and to the antichrist**).

¹³ <u>For you have said in your heart:</u> 'I will ascend into heaven, I will exalt my throne above the stars of God; I will also sit on the mount of the congregation. **Isaiah 14:13**, the mount of the congregation; the name is from the Babylonian religion. It was a mythical mountain that had its top in heaven and its roots go down to the "holy deep". It was called by them, "the mighty mountain of Bel". It was the place that satan claimed would be his launching platform to reach above the stars of God.

It is interesting to note the similarities between the tower of Babel and the boast of the devil; both desired to have a united dominion, both intended to reach even unto heaven by means of their labor, and both were confounded in their work by the judgment of God.

Mountains in the Bible always signify kingdoms. The seven mountains that the woman sits on in **Revelation 17:9-10 are** seven kings or kingdoms that the woman rules over. In **Daniel 2:35,** Daniel saw a stone cut without hands that destroyed the image and became a mountain so great that it filled the whole earth, this of course means the kingdom of Christ on earth, **Isaiah 9:6.** That kingdom will have no end.

In **Revelation 17:12** John is told of ten kings who will receive a kingdom for a short period with the antichrist-mahdi. The woman, who is ancient, will have seven kingdoms at her feet that she rules over. I believe that this is the Sunni nations to the south of Babylon. They will allow the antichrist to rise to rule over them, but will not know that his true intent is to destroy them.

He will have ten kings, men who will rule over literal nations, but who will only have one desire and that is to please the antichrist-mahdi.

They will perform his will and make war on the woman and destroy her. This speaks of the coming civil war in Islam.

A purging is constantly referred to by Muhammad. He believed only the purest of the pure could expect Allah's help, therefore anytime he lost at war it was because Allah was not pleased with the people. They were not Muslim enough for Allah and needed a purging by defeat to teach them.

The antichrist will purge Islam and then set his sights on destroying Israel. So it will be ten kings against seven. Ten nations allied with the antichrist-mahdi against seven who are only nominally allied with him. **Isa 14:20 because thou hast destroyed thy land, and slain thy people.** Many millions of Muslims will perish at the hands of their fellow Muslims in order to make the kingdom of antichrist pure enough to take on Israel. It is clear that the war will be over quick and that the losers will receive no mercy. The mahdi will strike with a continuous stroke, **Isaiah 14:6.** Any ruler who instisted on ruling alongside the Mahdi will be destroyed because only one can rule and the devil will not share power and neither will his puppet ruler.

On the farthest sides of the north; (Many preachers say that the devil tried to de-throne God, that is not possible, what he did try to do was exalt himself to equal status with God, something only Jesus has. This passage has a double meaning in that the antichrist will have the devils desire for supremacy over others. It is Muslim teaching that in Heaven there will be some exalted above others.)

[14] *I will ascend above the heights of the clouds; **I will be like** the Most High.'* (Remember Paul said that the antichrist would sit in the temple of God showing himself to be God. This speaks of the mountain, that is, the kingdom of the antichrist being above all others).

[15] *Yet you shall be brought down to Sheol, to the lowest depths of the Pit.* **(Again God says that the beast will go to hell).**

[16] ***"Those who see you will gaze at you, and consider you, saying: 'is this the man who made the earth tremble, who shook kingdoms,*** **(the devil is not a man, so this is referring to the antichrist).**

[17] ***Who made the world as a wilderness and destroyed its cities, which did not open the house of his prisoners?'*** **(The antichrist will destroy so many cities and people that it will be unimaginable.**

27

Notice the people; these people are in hell, yet they see, hear and recognize each other.)

[18] *"All the kings of the nations, All of them, sleep in glory, Everyone in his own house;* (**House in Hebrew means dungeon**).

[19] *But you are cast out of your grave Like an abominable branch,* (**he will not be buried but cast bodily into hell**) *Like the garment of those who are slain, Thrust through with a sword, Who go down to the stones of the pit, Like a corpse trodden underfoot.*

[20] ***You will not be joined with them in burial,*** (the antichrist will not be buried, he will be cast alive into hell) *because you have destroyed your land and slain* **your people.** *The brood of evildoers shall never be named.* (**Here we see that the antichrist will destroy his own, the Muslims, and his own land, perhaps meaning Mecca.**)

[21] *Prepare slaughter for his children because of the iniquity of their fathers, lest they rise up and possess the land, and fill the face of the world with cities."* (**God shows us the intent of the antichrist and his followers, to posses the land, Israel, and to fill the earth, that is, to conquer the world for Islam**).

[22] *"For I will rise up against them,"* *says the Lord of hosts,* *"And cut off from Babylon the name and remnant, and offspring and posterity,"* *says the Lord.* (**I will explain the Babylon connection later in the book**).

[23] *"I will also make it a possession for the porcupine, and marshes of muddy water; I will sweep it with the broom of destruction,"* *says the Lord of hosts.* (**The city of Babylon is still in existence today, but not in its former glory. This refers to somewhere else; somewhere that has the spirit of Babylon.**)

[24] *The Lord of hosts has sworn, saying, "Surely, as I have thought, so it* **shall come to pass, And as I have purposed, so it shall stand:** (**No man can stop the plan of God, He will do as He said**).

[25] *That I will break the Assyrian in My land, And on My Mountains tread him underfoot.* (**The Lord Jesus will personally tread the antichrist underfoot, fulfilling in part God's promise to Eve concerning her seed crushing the serpents head with His heel**). *Then his yoke shall be removed from them, and his burden removed from their shoulders.* (**Here the antichrist is again referred to as the Assyrian.**)

Micah 5:5

And this One shall be peace. **(The One here is Jesus the branch)**
When the Assyrian comes into our land, **(Israel)**
And when he treads in our palaces, (the only time Jesus will fight against an Assyrian is at the battle of Armageddon)

Micah 5:6

They shall waste with the sword the land of Assyria,
And the land of Nimrod at its entrances;
Thus He shall deliver us from the Assyrian,
When he comes into our land, **(Israel)**
and when he treads within our borders. **(Once again the antichrist is referred to as the Assyrian).**

Daniel 4:16

Let his heart be changed from that of a man,
*Let him be given the heart of a **beast,***
   And let seven times pass over him. **(7 years is the length of the tribulation. Here we see that the devil will put into his heart the evil thoughts he thinks. Just as Judas was deceived, so will the antichrist be.)**

In **Daniel 2:36-45** the great image that Nebuchadnezzar saw was a succession of kingdoms that should come. The head of gold was the Babylonian kingdom that was then in its zenith. The chest and two arms of silver were the Medes and Persians that later conquered Babylon. The belly and thighs that were of brass was the kingdom of Greece. The legs of iron were the kingdom of Rome.

There are two main points that I want to make about this image; first about the toes. They are mingled. In the Hebrew/Chaldee this is the word **Arab.** This speaks of a kingdom that will be of Arabs. The reason many do not believe this is because the legs of iron are definitely the Roman Empire, so the feet must be a revived Roman Empire.

The real problem here is that only four kingdoms are believed to be spoken about by Daniel. Actually if you read it you will see that he makes a distinction between the feet and the legs. The feet are a fifth kingdom that will rise in the "last days", which is the literal meaning of the dreams. In the days of these kings, vs. 44, shall God establish a kingdom that will crush all other kingdoms and it will fill the entire earth.

This is the second point that needs to be made; this happens in the days of these kings. Which kings is Daniel speaking about? The ten kings represented by the ten toes. They will be as strong as iron which means that they can not be broken. Yet they will be at constant odds with each other and not able to stick together.

Notice also that all five parts of the image are still connected when God establishes the kingdom of Christ on earth. This means that the empires of the world will be united with the ten kings to attack Israel at Armageddon. They will all be completely crushed by Jesus at the battle.

Daniel 7:8

While I was thinking about the horns, another horn, a little horn, came up among them. It uprooted three of the other horns. This horn had eyes like human eyes and a mouth that spoke impressive things. (**This is referring to the antichrist. Daniel saw that it uprooted three leaders and took over their nations. He has eyes, which speak of wisdom and a mouth which was gifted by satan himself to deceive the world**).

Daniel 7:11 *I continued to watch because of the impressive words that the horn was speaking. I watched until the animal was killed. Its body was destroyed and put into a raging fire.* (**Again, the Lord says that the antichrist will be thrown bodily into hell**).

Daniel 7:19-21 *Then I wanted to know the truth about the fourth animal, which was so different from all the others. It was very terrifying and had iron teeth and bronze claws. It devoured and crushed its victims, and trampled whatever was left.* (**Notice the nature of the antichrist, he devours and crushes**).

20I also wanted to know about the ten horns on its head and about the other horn that had come up and made three of the horns fall out. (The antichrist will uproot three leaders and take control of their nations.) ***That horn had eyes and a mouth that spoke impressive things.*** *It appeared to be bigger than the others*

. 21I saw that horn making war against the holy people and defeating them.
(**The holy people referred to here are the Jews**)

Daniel 7:24-25

The ten horns are ten kings that will rise to power from that kingdom. *Another king will rise to power after them. He will be different from the kings who came before him,* **and he will humble three kings.**
25He will speak against the Most High God, oppress the holy people of the Most High, **and plan to change the appointed times and laws.**
The holy people will be handed over to him for a time, times, and half of a time (**3.5 years. Again this speaks of the antichrist conquering Israel at least in part. Muslims desire to change the counting of days and years to correspond to their reckoning as opposed to the Julian calendar.**)
Daniel 8:8-14 *The male goat became very important. But when the goat became powerful, his large horn broke off. In its place grew four horns. They corresponded to the four winds of heaven.*
*9Out of one of the horns came a small horn. It gained power over the **south, the east,** and the beautiful land.* (**Meaning Israel**)
10It continued to gain power until it reached the army of heaven. It threw some of the army of heaven, the stars, down on the ground and trampled them.
11Then it attacked the commander of the army so that it took the daily burnt offering from him and wrecked his holy place. (**This again speaks of him killing the two witnesses and stopping the daily sacrifices in the temple. He will clean the temple of any Jewish things and replace them with Muslim items and a statue dedicated to himself.**)
*12In its rebelliousness it was given an army to put a stop to the daily burnt offering. It **threw truth on the ground.*** (**Jesus is the way, the TRUTH and the life, he will attack the truth about Jesus**) *The horn was successful in everything it did.* (**The antichrist will defeat the two witnesses and their followers in battle; he will at that time make the nation of Israel subservient to him**)
13Then I heard a holy one speaking. Another holy one said to the one who was speaking, "How long will the things in this vision—the daily burnt

offering, **the destructive rebellion, the surrender of the holy place,** *and the* **trampling of the army**—*take place?"*

14He told me, "For 2,300 evenings and mornings **(3.5 years)***. Then the holy place will be made acceptable to God."*

26"And after the sixty-two weeks **(483 years from Cyrus' proclamation to rebuild the city of Jerusalem)**

Messiah shall be cut off, but not for Himself; **(this important passage puts the exact date when Christ died and says that Jesus died for others, proving the Bible and Christianity)**

27Then he **(the antichrist)** *shall confirm a covenant with many for one week ;(* **7 years)**

But in the middle of the week **(3.5 years)**

He shall bring an end to sacrifice and offering. **(When he kills the two prophets in Jerusalem and retakes the Temple Mount).**

And on the wing of abominations shall be one, who makes desolate, **(The abomination of desolation spoken of by Jesus will most likely be the statue of the antichrist that will speak).**

These passages in Daniel make it clear that the antichrist will make war on Israel after **3.5 years.** During the first **3.5 years** of the tribulation he will not be able to totally conquer Israel due to the protection afforded by the two witnesses.

As soon as the two witnesses are killed he will defeat Israel and subdue it. This does not mean that he will destroy it, but he will definitely defeat it. From the point that the abomination is placed in the Temple, whoever is watching and listening will know he has about 3.5 years till Jesus returns.

It is pretty easy to see that the antichrist will be a **religious figure.** The cleansing of the temple mount means that Israel will be reinstituting sacrifices during the first **3.5 years.** It will be in the middle of the tribulation that the **antichrist Mahdi** will come with the false prophet who claims to be Jesus to kill Elijah and Enoch as well as their followers.

It is at this time (the second half of the tribulation) that the antichrist will set himself up in the temple of God showing himself to be God, **2 Thessalonians 2:4.** He will receive and demand to be worshipped.

The Second Rider; 6:4, The Second Seal; Religious War.

Revelation 6:4 Mt.24:6, Mk.13:8, Lk.21:10

4 (GW) A second horse went out. It was fiery red. Its rider was given the power to take peace away from the earth and to make people slaughter one another. So he was given a large sword.

Identification of the second rider.

Jesus said that false Christ and false prophets would arise, and that many would come in His name saying that He is Christ. One of the fundamental teachings of Islam is that Jesus was the last prophet before Muhammad and that **He failed in His mission, was never crucified,** so therefore He must return to earth to **assist the Mahdi.** Their version of Jesus will not have scars from the crucifixion; according to them he was never crucified.

The devil is already laying the groundwork for his eventual rise. Every prophecy in the Koran is an exact opposite of the true prophecies in the Bible; it's almost like looking at a reverse image. Religion is the glue that holds these people together. Faith in the words of a man, and thru the man the devil is their strength.

The false prophet who will be the Muslim Jesus will promote worship of the antichrist that the Muslims call the Mahdi. It will be in the heart of this man to fulfill all the Muslim prophecies spoken about him. He will believe at least in part that he really is Jesus. Deceiving and being deceived the two of them will lead the world down a religious journey to hell.

Note here the Islamic view spoken by Muhammed:

There is no prophet between me and him, that is, Jesus. He will descent **(to the earth).** When you see him, recognize him: a man of medium height, reddish fair, wearing two light yellow garments, looking as if drops were falling down from his head though it will not be wet. He will fight the people for the cause of Islam. He will break the cross **(abolish Christianity),** kill swine **(kill the Jews),** and abolish jizyah **(the tax non Muslims must pay, because he will kill all non-Muslims).** Allah will perish all religions except Islam **(This is still the plan of Islam, the destruction of all other religions except Islam).** He will destroy the Antichrist **(the prophets in Jerusalem, Elijah and Enoch)** and will live on the earth for forty years and then he will die. The Muslims will pray over him. (Sunan Abu Dawud, Book 37, No. 4310)

He will kill the prophet in Jerusalem.

"He then reported that Allah's Messenger said: The Dajjal **(the prophet in Jerusalem)** will appear in my Ummah **(The Ummah refers to his time as prophet, which still exist because his words still rule over the Muslims)** and he will stay **(in the world)** for forty -- I cannot say whether he meant forty days, forty months or forty years. Allah will then send Jesus, son of Mary. He **(Jesus according to Muslims)** will chase him and kill him **(the prophet in Jerusalem).** Every non-believer who smells the odor of his body will die and his breath will reach as far as he is able to see. **(Notice that death and killing are what this man will be known for).** He will then search for him **(Dajjal, according to the Muslims prophecy, the man they call the antichrist will be a hairy man. That is exactly how the Bible describes Elijah)** until he catches hold of him at the gate of Ludd **(Jerusalem)** and kills him."

You see how the Koran has got it completely backwards. It says the exact opposite of the Bible.

Here we have the second rider who **accompanies the first rider.** For some reason most expositors treat these riders as if they are totally independent of each other. It is clear that the work of the first rider causes the others to be able to come forth. In other words, it is the antichrist' ascension and the subsequent worship of him that causes so many millions to die.

This horse is red, the color of blood. All thru the Word blood is used of Sanctification, purity, guilt and sin. Sanctification and purity are for the believer, guilt and sin are for the unbeliever.

The policy of the first rider is to gain power thru lies and deception. The result is the bloodbath that will follow. According to Muslim doctrine, as we've shown, their version of Jesus will appear at a time when the Muslim world will be divided and at war with itself.

Then, **according to them,** the Mahdi will conquer many Muslim nations before turning his sights on Jerusalem. At that time he will be assisted by their Jesus. It is their Jesus who will actually kill the two prophets who will be in Jerusalem and will cover his sword in blood. This false Jesus is a cold blooded religious killer. **The real Jesus gave His life; the false one takes life.**

He will have supernatural power and will be able to do miracles in the presence of the antichrist according the Bible, **(Second Thessalonians 2:9-10)** *even he, whose coming is according to the **working of Satan** with **all power** and **signs** and **lying wonders,** [10] and with **all deceit** of unrighteousness for them that perish; because they received not **the love of the truth,** that they might be saved).* There is every reason to believe that this man will not appear until midway thru the Tribulation. As I've said, he will not show any wounds from the crucifixion because according to Muhammad, Jesus was never crucified.

According to Islam, the two prophets who will be Gods witnesses in Jerusalem will be **who they call antichrist-Dajjil**. I will have more to say about this later on.

[4 (GW)] *A second horse went out. It was fiery red. Its rider was given the power to take peace away from the earth and to make people slaughter one another. So he was given a large sword.*

Verse four speaks of the coming **religious war** in Islam. There has always been a smoldering hatred between the Shiites and Sunnis. The false Jesus will initiate a religious war that will draw in all religions. Remember that there is a spirit that precedes the man. This means that the spirit will be stirring people to kill one another before the second rider is manifested to the world. We know that the fake Jesus will show up in the middle of the tribulation. But the spirit behind him will already have paved the way before him.

How do you make people want to destroy each other? The answer is you have to bring religion into the picture. People will gladly kill over religion when they wouldn't do it for any other reason. When I speak of religion, I am not talking about having a relationship with Jesus Christ; I am talking about religious dogma that is either man made or satanic in its origin.

Islam is noted as much for blood as it is for anything. Every day on the news we are subjected to images of faithful Muslims killing each other. It has always been a warring religion. Even today the struggle continues with violent repercussions. He will take peace from the earth. No peace treaty will stand up to his religious edict.

Understand this; a good Muslim is one who does exactly what Muhammad did. And what did Muhammad do? He killed all who opposed his religion and his rule. He personally fought in 63 conflicts. He sanctioned assassinations and murder.

The second rider is war and bloodshed. He will bring war on a much larger scale than has been seen in the Middle East to that time. I believe he will instill religious hatred into the mix. What have basically been wars of aggression will now become war for the cause of Islam and God.

Dr. Kamal Nait-Zerrad is quoted here. **"For Islam, the Christian or Jewish Non-Muslim Can Only Be a Dhimmi, an infidel.** The fact is that Islam never foresaw a situation in which it would be in the minority. So long as one has not understood this, one cannot understand the Islamist movements. This is symptomatic of the Muslim vision of man, of human relations, and of other religions. Fighting against infidels is commanded in the Koran in these words [9:29]: 'Fight those who do not believe in Allah and in the last day, who do not forbid that which Allah and his Messenger declared forbidden, and who do not practice the religion of truth, among those who have received the Scripture! Fight them until they pay the jizya (poll tax), directly, when they are humiliated.'

The jizya is reserved only for those who have the Scripture - that is, Jews, Christians, and to a lesser extent, Zoroastrians. As for the others - pagans, animists, free-thinkers, agnostics, and atheists - **they have no other recourse but to convert to Islam or die.** "The study of the Koran allows one to point to the potential for intolerance that emerges from it and its outdated conception of law and justice. In essence, human rights have evolved in the direction of greater respect for man and his physical integrity. Some speak of a new interpretation of the Koran that is adapted to modern times.

However, the political, social, or moral concepts in the Koran are intangible, **and the Muslim cannot modify them or reject a part of them without being accused of** heresy - unless [such modification] comes from a recognized authority."

I want you to see how even a man who disagrees with his own peoples teaching despairs of any significant change taking place without serious repercussion. Fear is as much a part of Islam as Mecca and Medina. The antichrist Mahdi will be able to institute change in Islam due to his recognized authority. Any who oppose his rule, especially the last 3.5 years of it, will suffer deadly consequences.

It is not that all Muslims are evil. What I am saying that any religion that suppresses thinking and reasoning is not of God. If you fear to question the Bible, you surely do not understand the nature of God. God is not afraid for you to ask Him a question. It does not mean that you doubt Him; it just means you are going to the source to get an answer. If you can't handle someone questioning your beliefs without getting mad, then you really don't believe them yourself.

The third seal; the black horse, the new economy

Revelation 6:5-6 Mt.24:7, Mk.13:8, Lk.21:11

5 (GW) When the lamb opened the third seal, I heard the third living creature say, "Go!" I looked, and there was a black horse, and its rider held a scale.

*6 I heard what sounded like a voice from among the four living creatures, saying, "A quart of wheat for a day's pay or three quarts of barley for a day's pay. **But do not damage the oil and the wine.**"*

Next we see a black horse. *The rider has control of the horse. He will control the world's economy. It is thru the oil that Islam has gained its wealth and power. It will be thru the oil that the antichrist Mahdi will control the world's economy. It's interesting to note something here about the color black. For Muslims the thought of one day flying the black flag over* *the White House makes them excited. The black flag is the flag of Islam. Every nation will be required to submit to Shari a, that is, Islamic law or face destruction.*

Black is the color associated with Muhammad, but the black flag of extremism also signifies revenge, revolution, war, and is reflected in the black headband or turban of a warrior going into battle. Islamic tradition teaches that there will be a call from the sky at the beginning of The Day, and an army will come forth out of Afghanistan wearing black headbands and carrying black banners. It was Muhammad who told Muslims that when they see the black flags they must join that army of men in a relentless march toward Jerusalem. It is this army that will pave the way for Imam Mahdi's kingdom to rule.

So it has been, and will continue to be, the ancient Islamic goal to have the black flag of Islam flying over the city of Jerusalem.

(Flag of Jihad, used by permission, see back page)

The following is an excerpt from a hadith, or oral teaching of Islam.

"In a similar prophecy, Muhammad said: The people of my Household will suffer a great deal after my death, and will be persecuted until a people **carrying black banners** will come out of the east (**region of Iraq or Iran**). They will instruct the people to do good, but the people will refuse; they will fight until they are victorious, and the people do as they asked, but they will not accept it from them until they hand over power to a man from my household (**the Mahdi-antichrist**). Then the earth will be filled with fairness, just as it had been filled with injustice. If any of you live to see this, you should go to him even if you have to crawl across ice."

The black flag is the color of the religion of the Mahdi, the antichrist. **It is the color of Islam.**

A prophecy in ancient Islamic tradition indicates a **black wind** will rise up at the beginning of "The Day" of judgment and then a great earthquake will shake the land so much that it will almost be swallowed up.

100 years ago people could not imagine anyone fighting for the land of Israel or the Middle East. It was waste land and barren. Yet God has known all along what He was doing. Now all wars seem to have something to do with the religions of the Middle East or the oil of the Middle East.

God knew how to bring Islam to the forefront; He put **the oil**, which is black, where the Muslims live! Desert land is now worth trillions of dollars. This gives the Arabs enormous clout and power. Financially they will be in a position to dictate world policy based on **oil.**

That's why the Word says, "Hurt not the oil", the oil will be the catalyst behind the antichrist' rise to dominance. Incidentally, **hurt not** in the Greek means "**to not do injustice to**".

It is impossible to explain the impact oil has on our society. Virtually everything that we use on a daily basis has something to do with oil. Plastics, gasoline for our cars, we need fuel for our power plants so we can have electricity; we need massive quantities of oil just to keep America going.

In the United States we consume an average of 10.25 quadrillion BTU's of energy every year growing, harvesting, packaging, shipping, refrigerating and preparing our food. Most of those BTU's come from oil. Without cheap oil we would literally be starving right now. We are already at the mercy of the oil producers, we just don't know it.

America imports an amazing 1,476,000,000,000 (1.476 trillion) dollars worth of oil per year! That is 58 percent of the oil we consume. By 2025 it is estimated that it will rise to about 68 percent. We have the military, but they have the power.

Sadly the people, who should be getting the benefits of our spending on oil, do not receive anything. I speak of the Arab people. While their leaders are getting more billions in the bank, they slip deeper into poverty of mind and body. Who do they blame for this? They blame America and Israel!

The economic impact of the oil monopoly will be the direct cause of hyperinflation in the rest of the world. The economies of entire nations will be brought to their knees because of the power of oil. There will be no choice except to pass the cost on to the consumers. The result will be sky high prices on bread and other staples of life. **Massive famines will be the result of these policies as entire nations can't pay the Muslim ransom.**

For an example of this policy, **look at the Sudan,** famine is exactly what they are using on their Muslim and Christian citizens to subdue them. Islam allows its followers to use any method at their disposal to subdue their enemies, no matter how cruel it may be.

In **Daniel 8:25**, we are told that the antichrist **will cause craft to prosper in his hands**. What this literally means is that he will cause deceit to prosper. By lying and falsehood he will establish his kingdom. In **Second Thessalonians 2:11**, Paul tells us that in the end time, **God will send upon the people a strong delusion, that they should believe a lie**. The literal translation of this verse is, "**the lie**".

There is only one truth, Jesus is the truth! There is one lie, told many different ways, namely this, that Jesus isn't the truth. This is the central core of Islam that Jesus wasn't Gods Son and He is not the way. People want to believe the lie because that clears them of personal guilt for rejecting Jesus. God will give them what they want, but it will not prosper them.

How is Islam taking over Europe and Russia?

There are really two answers; **one is the native population having abortions, the other is by Muslims having so many babies.** Abortion worldwide is having a devastating effect. There are around 46 million babies aborted worldwide every year. That comes to about 126,000 per day. In Russia (which legalized abortions in 1920) the native Slavic population is actually decreasing in numbers as a direct result of their having so many abortions.

The Russian Muslims, who do not allow abortions, are growing in numbers. Since 1989 Russia's Muslim population has increased by

40%. By the year 2050 Russia will be predominately Muslim. Russian women are having two abortions for every live birth. That means that two-thirds of Russia's children are killed before they are born.

Russia's overall population is shrinking by about one million every year. The fertility rate for Russia's native Slavs is about 1.5 per family. It takes about 2.4 per family to sustain the present population of about 142 million. The average Russian Muslim however is reproducing at the rate of <u>six children per woman</u>. Some families are having upwards of <u>ten children per woman.</u>

What this means is that the Muslims will one day take over Russia without having to fire one shot. They are going to overwhelm by virtue of superior numbers.

The Muslims are well aware of the changes taking place. In fact, they are encouraging their people to have as many babies as possible. Many Muslim men around the world are taking multiple wives to accomplish their goal of global domination.

Osama Bin Laden came from such a family. His mother was only one of his dad's wives. His dad married as many as 22 times, though only four at a time as Sharia law directs. Osama was only one of his estimated 55 children. Bin Laden himself has married at least five women and has many children of his own.

France, England and all of Europe will be Muslim dominated by the middle of the 21st Century. Already France is caving into the pressure exerted by their Muslim citizens. The recent riots and anarchy in Paris were proof that the government has lost control of whole sections of the country. The only way that the police could regain control was by allowing the Muslims to police themselves. French police refused to enter Muslim enclaves. In effect, they are allowing portions of France to be governed by Islamic law.

Today in England there are Mosque being built where once there were thriving churches. Large parts of the country are now turning to Islam.

So the obvious question must be asked; what has happened to the church? The churches have been dying in England because so many of them compromised with the world so much that it became too much like the world. People who were looking for something solid couldn't find it in most churches. The percentage of people who are practicing

Christians has dropped while abortion totals have risen. As England and the rest of Europe get older, Muslim communities are getting younger.

The only answer for Europe is a revival in the church. Unless the church returns to the Lord these trends will continue. By the time the world realizes what is happening it may be too late. The church of the Lord Jesus Christ is the most powerful force on the planet. The entire world wants to see a powerful church, one in which the Gospel is preached without compromise. I repeat the world wants to hear the truth preached. They want strength from Gods people. God still will confirm the Word with signs following if we will only preach the Word.

The fourth seal; the pale horse, pestilence and death.

Revelation 6:7-8 Mt.24:7, Mk.13:8, Lk.21:11

7 (GW) *When the lamb opened the fourth seal, I heard the voice of the fourth living creature say, "Go!"*
8 I looked, and there was a pale horse, and its rider's name was Death. Hell followed him. They were given power over one-fourth of the earth to kill people using wars, famines, plagues, and the wild animals on the earth.

The direct cause from the policies of the antichrist will be that **Death and Hades**, the grave, will kill **one fourth of mankind**. At today's population this would be about **2 billion people!** And how will they die? The answer is in **verse 8; WAR, FAMINE, DEATH, AND BEAST OF THE EARTH.** Beast in **Revelation 6:8** means a **poisonous thing**. In other words, either by chemicals or other means, poison will kill millions. The fact that the horse was pale means sickness. Some have suggested that the word "chloros" in the Greek means green. In this case as well as many others it means withered, like a dead leaf.

Here is another Muslim prophecy; "before the one who will arise (their Mahdi, the antichrist), there will be red death and white death; there will be locusts at their usual time and at their unusual time like the colors of blood. As for red death, that is (from) the sword, while white death is (from) plague."

The devil wants them to trust in the Koran, so he takes some of scripture and twist it.

Pestilence and disease will be widespread and many will die from not just diseases, **but poisons.** Aids and other killer viruses are going to get worse and worse. New things will spring up deadlier than the last.

At the **beginning** of the birth pangs, these things will be happening. Yet people will choose to ignore the clear signs all around them. War, famine and death on every side do not really move us. We see worse at the movies and on T.V. Yet the closer we get to the end the worse these things are going to get, and the more frequent the attacks will come.

Even though the church is not going thru the tribulation, it will see the signs of the end, the **beginnings of sorrows**. When Jesus spoke of the "tribulation of those days" it is clear that He was talking about something different than the period we call the "great tribulation".

The Greek word that is used means pressure, or heaviness. I firmly believe that the church will indeed be forced to fight the pressure of the last days. But that is not the same as the great tribulation period. It is a time when men's hearts will fail them for fear from looking after the things that are coming on the earth.

At the very time that the church should be pulling out all the stops to tell people about Jesus, it is instead arguing and compromising. I fear that the welfare mentality has taken over the church of the Living God. Sacrifice is just an old fashioned word anymore. The church refuses to do without luxuries to see souls saved.

The fifth seal; persecution, many will grow cold and many will deny Jesus.

Rev. 6:9-11 Mat.24:9, Mk.13:9, Lk.21:12.

9 (GW) When the lamb opened the fifth seal, I saw under the altar the souls of those who had been slaughtered because of God's word and the testimony they had given about him.

¹⁰ They cried out in a loud voice, "Holy and true Master, how long before you judge and take revenge on those living on earth who shed our blood?"

¹¹ Each of the souls was given a white robe. They were told to rest a little longer until all their coworkers, the other Christians, would be killed as they had been killed.

All thru church history there have been persecutions against the believers. **Some people don't realize this, but there have been more martyrs killed in the past 100 years than at any other time in our history.** Communism and Islam are the two main causes of persecution. The devil is trying his best to stamp out the church, yet all he is doing is fanning the flames higher and hotter.

Islam in particular is violently antichristian. There is no room for Christianity in their world. They do what Muhammad taught them to do; they kill everyone who disagrees with the Koran.

The very word "Islam" **means to submit.** Muhammad taught that the entire world would submit to Allah or die. Muslims teach in their schools and in their mosques that one day all Jews and Christians will either submit to Islam or they will be killed.

Obviously then, persecution will lead to the beheading of many saints. In America right now we have Mosque teaching people that Jihad against Christians and Jews is every Muslims sacred duty. Saudi Arabia is spending billions of dollars to indoctrinate our youth in colleges to be Muslim. Remember, according to Islam, all Christians are deceived.

If Muhammad was right, then Christ was wrong.

Muslims will tell you that the New Testament is a corrupted document and that only the Koran is the word of God. They will never accept the validity of the Bible. Anyone who disagrees will receive **the preferred method of execution, beheading.** In verse 11 we are told that there would be many more martyrs during the tribulation period.

How true is the New Testament?

Let's settle something right up front; the New Testament is not a corrupted text. There are over **5,000 individual manuscripts** or pieces of manuscript in existence right now. **They all agree with the text we have today.** Not one of the 27 books we have in the New Testament has any discrepancy in them.

On top of that, we have the writings of the early church fathers. Their writings quote directly **over 99% of the New Testament**. There is nothing to prove the Muslim statement that our texts are corrupted. They just don't want to accept the truth because it would conflict with the word of Muhammad, something that **the Koran doesn't allow anyone to do.**

If the Muslims were correct and Muhammad was correct, then there should be thousands of other gospels or at least fragments from the same time period in existence. Muhammad claimed that in his day there were books from both the old and new testaments to support his claims. **Where are those books?** If they were the Word of God as he claims, then why haven't the Muslims saved at least one copy?

The only things they can quote from to support their ideas are the Gnostic Gospels of the second century and later. Something else that you should know, Muhammad was illiterate; he couldn't have studied the Gospels or the Hebrew Old Testament.

The only things Muhammad seems to know of are old stories and fables that he incorporated into his religion. Many of his teachings concerning Jesus are from the Gnostic teachings of the second and third centuries.

These false teachings were never accepted by the church. If Islam was to allow anyone to examine their text the way Christians allow anyone to examine ours, **Islam would fade from the pages of history in a generation.**

Every person who reads the Bible is instructed to *"Come now, and let us reason together, saith the LORD:* **Isaiah 1:18"**. The Dead Sea scrolls also validate the Old Testament books. There hasn't been one thing changed in those books either. God has protected His Word as only He could. It is reasonable to expect God to be able to protect His Word isn't it? **Psalms 119:89,** *forever Oh Lord, Thy Word is established in Heaven.* God has not lost the Word! He still has the original and has kept it for us.

Chapter four

The Rapture Of The Church

The sixth seal; the rapture of the church

Revelation 6:12-17 *I watched as the lamb opened the sixth seal. A powerful earthquake struck. The sun turned as black as sackcloth made of hair. The full moon turned as red as blood.* (This happens at the beginning of the tribulation).
13 *The stars fell from the sky to the earth like figs dropping from a fig tree when it is shaken by a strong wind.* (A meteor shower).
14 *The sky vanished like a scroll being rolled up. Every mountain and island was moved from its place.* (This will be a worldwide shaking. Every person on Earth will see, hear or feel the effects of the rapture. In other words, God will let them know who is really in control)
15 *Then the kings of the earth, the important people, the generals, the rich, the powerful, and all the slaves and free people hid themselves in caves and among the rocks in the mountains.* (It is amazing that even an atheist will pray when he is scared enough!)
16 *They said to the mountains and rocks, "Fall on us, and hide us from the face of the one who sits on the throne and from the anger of the Lamb,* 17 *because the frightening day of their anger has come, and who is able to endure it?"* (Their anger; meaning Jesus and the Fathers anger).
Luke 23:30 *and they shall begin to say to the mountains, Fall on us! And to the hills, cover us!* (These are Jesus' words).
Isaiah 2:10 *Enter into the rock, and hide thee in the dust, for fear of the Lord and for the glory of His Majesty.*

Isaiah 2:19 *And they shall go into the holes of the rocks, and into the caves of the earth for fear of Jehovah and for the glory of His majesty, when He arises to shake the earth terribly.*
Isaiah 2:21 *to go into the clefts of the rocks, and into the tops of the ragged rocks, for fear of Jehovah and for the glory of His majesty, when He arises to shake the earth terribly.*

Notice in Isaiah and Luke it also says that they shall hide in the mountains and caves for fear. Also Isaiah says that God "arises to shake the earth terribly!" Literally it means a monstrous earthquake. **This happens at the beginning of the Tribulation.**

On the day Jesus died, at the precise moment, the earth quaked. On the day the church leaves the earth, it quakes again. We should be warning the world. They have no idea what is coming! This world and the fashion of it are about to pass away. Jesus said it would come upon the earth like the sudden labor pains on a woman. In other words, suddenly and without warning it will hit.

There is something here that needs to be explained in detail. **The first five seals are already opened.** In **1John 2:18** John says; *little children, it is the last time. And just as you have heard that antichrist is coming,* **even now many antichrists have risen up, from which we know that it is the last hour.** So we see that in John's day the spirit of antichrist **was already loosed**. There have also been great persecutions against the church and many martyrs for Christ. In fact, it is fairly easy to point out things that prove the first five seals have been opened already.

What we are waiting on is the sixth seal; the number of man. As man was created on the sixth day, he will be redeemed completely at the opening of the sixth seal. I firmly believe that the evidence is there for anyone to see that the first five seals have been opened for some time. The point I wish to make is that the spirits behind these things will only get stronger and stronger as the Day of Judgment nears.

God is allowing these things certain leeway to do what He has said they could do. The pressure of life is only going to get worse as the end gets closer. If you think life is somehow going to line out I have bad news for you; Jesus is coming and the world you know is about to end.

There is a direct link to Jesus' description of the rapture and Johns'.

In Matthew 24:29-31, Mark 13:24-27 and Luke 21:25-28, Jesus described the scene **before, during** and **after** the rapture of the church. John describes the very same things in **Revelation 6:12-17**.

Here are a summary of the total descriptions.

1. *The sun will be darkened*
2. *The moon will become dark*
3. *The stars of heaven will fall*
4. *Great sign in heaven, (John says the heavens roll up like a scroll).*
5. ***Every one** will see the **SIGN** of the Son of Man in Heaven.*
6. *All nations shall mourn, John adds further the words of **Hosea 10:18, Isaiah 2:10,19&21** and of Jesus found in **Luke 23:30**, that all men feared and tried to hide in the rocks and mountains out of fear of the Judgment of God.*
7. *Then the trumpet sounds. At which time the angels are sent to gather the elect from one end of heaven to the other. **This is the rapture.***
8. *There is one more sign of note: at the time of the rapture, John says there will be a **massive worldwide earthquake in verse 12.** This agrees precisely with **Isaiah chapter 2:19&21**. This will be a terrible quake, making the whole world fear greatly.*

When the Bible speaks about the rapture it uses the Greek word "parousia" which means presence. It is only used in connection with the rapture. Usually it is translated as "coming" such as in this passage; **1 Thes. 4:13-17** *But I do not want you to be ignorant, brethren, concerning those who have fallen asleep, (The correct translation should read, "Those who have died,")* *lest you sorrow as others who have no hope.* **14For if we believe that Jesus died and rose again, even so God will bring with Him those who sleep in Jesus.** 15*For this we say to you by the word of the Lord, that we who are alive and remain until the **coming** of the Lord will by no means precede those who are asleep.* 16*For the Lord Himself will descend from heaven with a shout, with the voice of an archangel, and with the trumpet of God. And the dead in Christ will rise first.* 17**Then we who are alive and remain shall be caught up together with them** *in the clouds to meet the Lord in the air. And thus we shall always be with the Lord.*

When Paul says we will meet the Lord in the "air" it literally means the lower atmosphere. Not above the clouds, but at cloud level. It is a sign that every eye shall see, but not every one will understand. Will the world watch us go up? I personally don't believe that they will but there will definitely be a sign of the rapture.

Here are the other places where Parousia is used; **1Thessalonians 3:13, 5:23, 2Thessalonians 2:1, James 5:7&5:8.** In every instance where it is used it refers to our being gathered to Him, the rapture.

Also read **1 Corinthians 15:51-58** for a description of the rapture. There is a teaching that the doctrine of the rapture is a new thing. The apostles would disagree with that. They were looking for Jesus to come back in their lifetime! Paul said, "We who are alive". He expected to see Jesus in his lifetime.

Johns View Of The Raptured Saints In Heaven

Rev. 7:9-17

*After these things I looked, **and behold, a great multitude which no one could number, of all nations, tribes, peoples, and tongues, standing before** (this great multitude was made up of all colors and peoples. There is a very specific word that is translated as "before" and that is the Greek word "enopion".*

It literally means in the face of. These people are in the very presence of the throne of God and in the presence of the Lamb.) ***The throne and before the Lamb,*** *clothed with* <u>white robes</u>, (Jesus said that he that overcame would be robed in white, the Throne is in Heaven) *with palm branches in their hands, 10and crying out with a loud voice, saying, "Salvation belongs to our God who sits on the throne, and to the Lamb!"*

11All the angels stood around the throne and the elders and the four living creatures, and fell on their faces before the throne and worshiped God, 12saying:" Amen! Blessing and glory and wisdom, thanksgiving and honor and power and might, Be to our God forever and ever. Amen."

13Then one of the elders answered, saying to me, "Who are these arrayed in white robes, and where did they come from?" 14And I said to him, "Sir, you know." So he said to me, **"These _are the ones who come out of the_ _great tribulation, and washed their robes and made them white in_ _the blood of the Lamb._** *(The fact that they came out of great tribulation will be dealt with a little further. Notice that they washed their robes in the blood of the Lamb, these all are Christians.)* **15** **Therefore they are before** **the throne of God,** *and serve Him day and night in His temple. And He who sits on the throne will dwell among them.* **(These are Christians,** **washed in the blood.)**

16 *They shall neither hunger anymore nor thirst anymore; the sun shall not strike them, nor any heat;* **17** **for the Lamb who is in the midst of** **the throne will** **shepherd them** **and lead them to** **living fountains of** **waters.**

And God will wipe away every tears from their eyes." **Reading these** **descriptions of these people leaves no doubt that they are the** **raptured saints.** The Lord has removed His church from the earth to the secret place of His pavilion, **Psalms 27:5** *For in the time of trouble He shall hide me in His shelter, in the secrecy of His tabernacle He shall hide me; He shall set me up on a rock.*

Mat 24:36-44

But of that day and hour no one knows, no, not the angels of Heaven, but only My Father. But as the days of Noah were, so shall be the coming of the Son of Man. For as in the days before the flood, they were eating and drinking, marrying and giving in marriage, **_until the day Noah entered_** **_into the ark_.** *And* **_they did not know_** *until the flood came and took them all away.* (The day that Noah entered the ark judgment came. 120 years of warning them meant nothing. We have also been warning people, have we done any better than Noah? Will the world know what is happening?) *So also will be the coming of the Son of Man. Then* **_two_** **_shall_** *be in the field;* **_the one shall be taken, and the other left. Two_** **_shall_** *be grinding at the mill; the* **_one shall be taken, and the other left._** (In Matthew and the following passage in Luke the Lord makes it clear that the rapture will surprise even the believers. The two walking, the two working and in Luke the two sleeping all were taken by surprise. The rapture will be sudden and unexpected!) *Therefore watch; for you do not know what hour your Lord comes. But know this that if the steward of the house had known in what watch the thief would come, he would have watched and would not have allowed his house to be dug through.*

*Therefore you also be ready, **for in that hour you think not, the Son of Man comes.*** (Don't let anyone try to convince you that they know the day or hour, no one will know.)

Luke 17:23-37
And they shall say to you, lo, here! Or, behold, there! Do not go away, nor follow. For as the lightning which lights up, flashing from the one part under heaven, and shines to the other part under heaven, so also shall the Son of Man be in His day. (Just as lightning flashes suddenly across the night sky, the rapture will flash suddenly. It will catch the world unprepared.)

But first He must suffer many things and be rejected of this generation. (Jesus constantly told them these truths that He would suffer and die and after three days would resurrect.)

*And as it was in the days of Noah, so it also shall be in the days of the Son of Man. They ate, they drank, they married wives, they were given in marriage, until **the day** that Noah entered into the ark; and the flood came and **destroyed them all.***

So also as it was in the days of Lot: they ate, they drank, they bought, they sold, they planted, and they built;

*But **the day Lot went out of Sodom,** it rained fire and brimstone from the heaven and **destroyed them all.***(Once again this says that at the moment of the rapture something terrible will happen. Jesus makes it as plain as possible. **We have to do a better job of warning the world**. They are not going to wake up and notice we are gone; they are going to wake up to hell on earth.) *Even so it shall be in the day when the Son of Man is revealed.*

In that day he who shall be on the housetop, and his goods in the house, let him not come down to take them away. And likewise, he who is in the field let him not return to the things behind.

Remember Lot's wife. Whoever shall seek to save his life shall lose it, and whoever shall lose his life shall preserve it. (Here Jesus speaks to those who are left behind. If that happens to be anyone reading this book, then pay attention. Life as you know it is over! You have missed the last boat out! Repent now!)

*I tell you, in that night **there shall be two in one bed, the one shall be taken, and the other shall be left.***

Two shall be grinding together, one will be taken, and the other left. Two shall be in the field, one will be taken, and the other left. And they answered and said to Him, __Where, Lord?__ And He said to them, __wherever the body is, there the eagles__ (Greek has "buzzards") ___will be gathered together.___

Jesus explained that some of the people would be taken, to which His disciples asked, __"Taken where?"__ His answer is simple, *"Wherever the carcass is, that's where the buzzards gather"*. In other words He said, *"Do not worry about the place; I will gather you to where you need to be."* Jesus is coming for a people who are looking for Him, is that you?

PROOF THAT THE RAPTURE WILL TAKE PLACE BEFORE THE GREAT TRIBULATION:

In first __Thessalonians 4:13-18__, Paul speaks to the saints concerning the rapture. He uses a word in verse 17 that is translated as "caught up". The Greek word is, "harpadzo". It means to "rescue from danger or destruction". It does not mean to rescue __"out of danger"__, but __"from danger"__. There is a big difference. To save me __from hell,__ Jesus did not bring me __out of hell__. To save me from the time of Jacobs's trouble, Jesus will not bring me out of it.

Another scripture to consider is __Rev. 3:10__ which states; *"because you have kept the Word of My patience, I also will keep you from the hour of temptation, which shall come upon the entire world, to try them that dwell upon the earth."* Again, He promises to keep us __from, not out of__ the wrath to come. Read also these scriptures; __1 Thessalonians 1:9-10, 5:8; Romans 5:9.__ Once again the language is that He will deliver us __from the wrath to come.__

The elder said, "Who come". This means in the Greek, __"who come now"__. Some say that this is the people who have died in the Lord over the last 2,000 years. But that is not what is intended by the reading in Greek. It means they just came out right now. In __1Thessalonians 4:13-17__ Paul teaches us that those who are now dead are in Christ waiting to be reunited with their bodies. In __2Corinthians 5:8__ he said that to be absent from the body was to be present with the Lord.

All sainted dead will be reunited with their bodies, even if their bodies are nothing more than dust. God knows where every atom is;

He can reassemble our parts together again. I have no problem donating my organs after I die. But I need to warn whoever gets my kidneys or heart or liver; when Jesus calls my name my body will reassemble. That means my whole body. So you had better be ready to lose what I have given you! That heart will disappear when the trumpet sounds!

Jesus told the Sadducees that "all live unto God, for He is not the God of the dead but of the living." Well God is not the God of the sleeping either. We know this, that when we see Him we shall be like Him. For we shall see Him as He is. Everyone who is with Him is alive and well and waiting to be joined with us in the clouds. For another picture of the rapture from the Old Testament look at **Exodus 19** where God called the people to sanctify themselves for the third day when God would descend to the top of the mountain (cloud level). **The earth quaked; the trumpet blew; and God called to the people. Only the chosen few went up at the trumpet blast.**

In **Revelation 7**, they are the blood washed believers-the true church! **Verse 14** says; *and washed their robes and made them white in the blood of the Lamb*. This is at the time before the tribulation starts. These believers are bought by the blood of the Lamb of God. They could be no one else except the redeemed church of the Living God. If they came out of the tribulation, were washed in the blood, and stayed with Jesus **then they are the church.**

17for the Lamb who is in the midst of the throne will shepherd them and lead them to living fountains of waters

The Good Shepherd of our souls will keep us and lead us, even in Heaven itself He does not leave us. We only have one thing to fear; the thought of facing Jesus without having done His will. Even the Good Shepherd will correct in love. The Bible says, *"It is a fearful thing to fall into the hands of the Living God"* **Hebrews 10:31.**

A deeper look at the rapture;

One of the teachings that confuse many people is the teaching of a great falling away. In **2 Thessalonians 2:3,** Paul says, *"Let no man deceive you by any means: for that day shall not come, except there come a falling away first."* For many years it has been taught that this refers to a great apostasy. In fact, the Greek word is apostasy. But the meaning of the word is not actually **"a falling away"** as is taught. Rather it means **"a departure"**.

While in certain passages of Greek it carries with it the meaning of falling away, in this particular verse it carries with it the definite article in Greek, which means to depart or a departure.

The church has always had a great apostasy; we have never had a time when the devil wasn't trying to lead us astray. Even in Paul's day, many were departing from the faith. In the middle ages the majority of people in the so-called Christian countries of Europe did not actually know or read the Bible.

In our own day we have countless so called Christians who are subverting people with their apostasy. What Paul was talking about was something different; something that needed no interpretation. When this happens everyone will know it. <u>What he says will happen first is a departure.</u>

Then that man of sin will be revealed. **After the departure, comes the revealing.** After the church is removed, the devil will have nothing hindering his plan. Then the antichrist will be free to start his conquest.

When the church leaves this earth, there will be a sudden, massive earthquake. It will jar the foundations of the mountains. The sea will roar according to Jesus. Men's hearts will fail them for fear. The sun will be black in the noon sky, which means that large amounts of smoke will fill the atmosphere. Many people will be killed.

There will be massive devastation on earth as cities will crumble. The more developed a nation is, the more it will suffer. The financial burden will then be overwhelming. No one will be able to buy or sell anything. I will say much more about the earthquake later but keep this in mind; no power means there will be no water.

Our inner cities are so dependant on daily supplies of fresh water that they wouldn't last any time without it. Without water or food, the animal instinct would take over. People will kill to survive. Most of our rivers are already polluted so badly that no one could drink from them without getting very sick. After the rapture people will have no choice but to drink.

If I am painting a grim picture it is only because that is the picture the Bible warns us about. God said in His Word in **Deuteronomy**

30:19. *"I call Heaven and earth to record today against you. I have set before you life and death, blessing and cursing. Therefore, choose life, so that both you and your seed may live."*

God is warning everyone and He isn't going to stop; repent quickly! Jesus never played games on earth; He always meant exactly what He said. He isn't playing games today either. Repent or perish. It is that simple.

The raptured church in Heaven.

The next scene John sees is of the **raptured church.** The picture is breathtaking. In verse nine John sees a great multitude, which no man could count. There are all nations, kindred's, peoples and tongues standing before the throne. The word translated "before" is the Greek word **"enopion"** which means "in the face of".

Some say that this is not the raptured saints. To that I simply ask, why not? Look at the description again. They are in the face of the Lamb, clothed in white robes, which were promised to whoever overcame in **chapter 3:5** they had palms in their hands and they cried "Salvation"!

Furthermore the angel explains who they are to John. These are they that have come out of great tribulation. "Come out" here means either to "go out, or to come out". It is clear that the meaning is that they have escaped great tribulation.

They have washed their robes and made them white in the blood of the Lamb. They are in the face of the throne, and serve Him day and night in His temple, **Rev. 3:12.**

God shall dwell among them, and they shall never hunger or thirst. Neither shall the sun or heat touch them. The Lamb Himself shall feed them, **Rev.3:20; 2:7; 2:17.** He shall lead them to living fountains of water and God Himself shall wipe away all tears from their eyes. That is as good of a description of the raptured saints as I have ever heard. These things are promised to the churches **if** they overcame in **chapters 2&3.**

After the rapture takes place, what will the church be doing?

1. The Judgment seat of Christ will take place in Heaven.

1 Cor. 3:11-15

For no other foundation can anyone lay than that which is laid, which is Jesus Christ. 12Now if anyone builds on this foundation with gold, silver, precious stones, wood, hay, straw, 13each one's work will become clear; for the Day will declare it, because it will be revealed by fire; and the fire will test each one's work, of what sort it is.(People will watch as their works are reviewed by the eyes of Jesus. Many will see all that they have done perish in ashes. Only those things that were done for the right reasons will survive the fire of the Lords gaze.) *14If anyone's work which he has built on it endures, he will receive a reward. 15If anyone's work is burned, he will suffer loss; but he himself will be saved, yet so as through fire.* Only Christians will be judged at this judgment.

1 Cor. 4:5. *Therefore judge nothing before the time,* **until the Lord comes,** *who will both bring to light the hidden things of darkness and* **reveal the counsels of the hearts.** *Then each one's praise will come from God.* (How can we know what is in someone's heart? **Proverbs 20:27** **The spirit of man is the lamp of Jehovah, _searching all the inward parts of the belly._** (The belly here means heart, the inner man. Your conscious self as well as your hidden self are clear to Him.**1Corinthians 2:10; for the Spirit searches all things, yea, the deep things of God.** *God searches our hearts constantly. He is always trying to move us to do things for the right reasons. No one will be without excuse before Him. He knows all!)*

2 Cor. 5:10 For we must all appear before the judgment seat of Christ *that each one may receive the things done in the body, according to what he has done, whether good or bad.*

Romans 14:10 *But why do you judge your brother? Or why do you show contempt for your brother?* **For we shall all stand before the judgment seat of Christ.**

Heb 4:12-13. *For the Word of God is living and powerful and sharper than any two-edged sword, piercing even to the dividing apart of **soul and spirit,*** (there is a difference between the soul and spirit; the soul is the area of the mind and the emotions. The spirit is the eternal part of each person.) And of the joints and marrow, and is a discerner of the ***thoughts and intents of the heart.*** (Here again God makes it clear; He knows why you do what you do.)

*Neither is there any creature that is not manifest in His sight, but all things are **naked and opened** to the eyes of Him with whom we have to do.* (No one wants to think that God sees us naked, but He can see thru anything! Even your heart is an open book to Him. You can't fool God! He always knows why you do what you do.)

The Bema Seat Judgment

The Judgment seat in the original Greek is the word Bema. The Bema was an elevated seat where during the athletic competitions the judge could sit and see the athletes' performances. From his vantage point he could see whether they competed according to the rules or not. The judge's verdict was final; there was no appeal. If he determined that you didn't win the race, then that was the ruling. The judge saw everything!

The Apostle Paul used a lot of athletic themes in his writings. In **1 Cor. 9:24-27** he writes;

Do you not know that those who run in a race all run, but one receives the prize? Run in such a way that you may obtain it. 25And everyone who competes for the prize is temperate in all things. Now they do it to obtain a perishable crown, but we for an imperishable crown. 26Therefore I run thus: not with uncertainty. Thus I fight: not as one who beats the air (he says he is not shadow boxing, his punches are meant to land).
*27But I discipline my body and bring it into subjection, lest, when I have preached to others, **I myself should become disqualified.***
Is it possible to be a reject? Could a Christian lose his salvation? Paul said that it was possible if we leave Christ. He taught that we can fall from grace.

Gal 5:4 *Ye are severed from Christ, ye who would be justified by the law; ye are fallen away from grace.* You can't fall from a place you have not been. To fall from grace means that you had obtained grace at one time.

For the time has come that judgment must begin in the house of God, **1 Peter 4:17** *For the time has come for judgment to begin at the* *house of God; and if it <u>begins with us first,</u> what will be the end of those who do not obey the gospel of God?*

The Judgment Seat is after the rapture **and in Heaven**, but **before the Marriage Supper**. We know it is before the Marriage Supper because seating at the dinner is by reward. Therefore the rewards are previous to the dinner.

Only Christians will be judged there. A lifetime of work and labor for the Lord that is not done for the right reasons from the heart will be burned to ashes in the sight of heaven. Jesus will look into each heart and disclose the motives and intents of the heart.

If that doesn't scare a Christian then something very bad is wrong with you. Everyone must keep a diligent watch over their heart to make sure that our motives are pure. What will it be like to have nothing to show for a lifetime's labor? I believe people will want to return to earth and have another chance to do what God commands them to do, but will not be allowed to.

2. The Marriage Supper of the Lamb will then take place in Heaven.

The Marriage Supper is a celebration feast!

<u>Heb 12:22</u> *but you have come to Mount Zion and to the city of the living God, the heavenly Jerusalem, and to* **<u>innumerable angels in festal gathering,</u>**

<u>Heb 12:23</u> *and to the assembly of the firstborn who are enrolled in heaven, and to God, the judge of all, and to the spirits of the righteous made perfect,*

<u>Heb 12:24</u> *and to Jesus, the mediator of a new covenant,*

<u>Luk 14:8-10</u> *When thou art bidden of any man to a wedding, sit not down in the highest room; lest a more honourable man than thou be bidden of him;*

And he that bade thee and him come and say to thee, Give this man place; and thou begin with shame to take the lowest room.

But when thou art bidden, go and sit down in the lowest room; that when he that bade thee cometh, he may say unto thee, Friend, go up higher: then shalt thou have worship in the presence of them that sit at meat with thee.

So we see that sitting will be by reward at the marriage supper. The more honored you are the closer to the King you will be. The whole hosts of Heaven are gathered to coronate the King! Angels and righteous men are there together to celebrate that glad day. Jesus will eat with us! What a glad day for the children of God. This will be a celebration like we have never seen.

Chapter five

The world after the rapture

1 Th 5:3 *For when they shall say, Peace and safety; then* **sudden destruction** *cometh upon them, as travail upon a woman with child; and they shall not escape. It is certainly not my desire that sudden destruction come on the earth; but it is coming whether we like it or not. As soon as people think safety has at last been achieved, the tribulation will start.*

What will convince them that peace has come? According to **Daniel 9:27** the antichrist will sign a peace accord with the Nation of Israel. Given our understanding of Mid-east politics this will be a momentous occasion. As many politicians have found out, peace is very elusive there.

Why would he make peace? I believe two reasons will force him to settle on a peaceful solution.

1. The entire financial world will be destroyed and he will need time to restore his military to where he can hope to destroy Israel.
2. The two witnesses will be in Jerusalem as soon as the rapture happens. They will be well able to destroy anyone who opposes them. The antichrist will need time to mount a successful war. His interest in the first 3.5 years of the tribulation will be on consolidating his political and financial empire.

America

There has never been a nation as blessed as America. We have the highest standard of living of any large industrialized nation. We have opportunities here that make the entire world envious. Yet in the midst of our plenty we have a great famine. It's not a famine of food; we have more than enough of that. It is a famine for the word of God.

We have God preached and sang about 24 hours a day on TV and radio. We have many churches all across the nation. Yet we don't have many preachers preaching the whole word. What are they preaching? Psychology, sociology, and self-help techniques that make the church feel better about themselves. The only problem with their doctrine is that the church is not ready for Jesus to come back!

If the church was preparing for the Lord to return, then they would be witnessing to everyone they met. They would give away unnecessary plunder if it kept them from doing the Masters will. Prayer would be the most important thing in their lives! The average American Christian prays less than 10 minutes a day. If that is all we are talking to God, then how can we really say that we love Him and are looking for Jesus' soon return? **Mark 13:37 (ASV),** *and what I say unto you I say unto all, Watch.* **America, wake up please!** Soon Jesus will show the difference in His people and the false worshippers of God. **Heb 12:25** *See that you do not refuse Him who speaks. For if they did not escape, those who refused him that spoke on earth, much more we shall not escape if we turn away from Him who speaks from Heaven,*

Heb 12:26 *whose voice then shook the earth; but now He has promised, saying, "Yet once more I will not only shake the earth, but also the heavens.* There is a shaking coming; are you ready?

Why Do The Nations Of The World Hate The United States?

Consider this quote from Arab TV and you will understand their thinking. "There is a phenomenon of Arabs and Muslims willing to die a martyr's death. They are willing to die, willing to blow themselves up, and this is what America fears. America has taken over the world with so – called globalization. It has taken over the world economically by means of the big banks; it has taken it over in the security sense by means of the treacherous regimes… and it has taken it over in the media sense by means of the mighty arms of the media, such as the Internet and satellite channels. **The only thing capable of ruining this globalization is armed actions against the embassies… as the American military is unbeatable (in direct confrontation)…**"

Consider this: what we call the Third World is in debt to our financiers a staggering 40% of their G.N.P. compound that at 20% interest (the current amount charged them) and you have them going deeper into debt than they can pay it out. Am I saying that the U.S is evil? **No I am not**. What I am saying is that we have allowed large multi-national banking institutions like the IMF to bring the world to the brink of collapse. The worst part of it is, we are the biggest debtor, to our own selves.

Another reason the world hates us is that we force all international transactions to be done in U.S dollars. While this sounds small it isn't. By forcing them to use our money, <u>we are then able to charge them interest on the use of the dollar.</u> **Basically we are taxing the world to finance our out of control spending.** This affects the Arab governments because of the transactions due to selling oil on the world markets. Our support for Israel causes them to hate us, but their forced taxation makes them hate us even more. The leaders of those nations do not want to give their money to us, only to have us turn around and give it to Israel.

Barring some unforeseen miracle, the world's debt will choke off any long term growth. Even today's robust economy is being held up by borrowing, not growth. The need to control spending has never been greater, yet the need to spend has never been greater either. If we don't spend, our economy and the world's economy will simply collapse overnight. We are on the brink of spending our way into oblivion and there appears to be no leader with the courage to do something about it.

I would like to show you a couple quotes: First is from the president of Nigeria, Obasanjo. "All that we had borrowed up to 1986 was $5 billion. We have paid about $16 billion back and we are still about $28 billion in debt on the original $5 billion."

The second quote comes from Gregory Palast. "The IMF offered Argentina a $20 billion bailout loan. This pushed their debt to a staggering $128 billion. Normal interest amounted to $27 billion annually. In other words, Argentina's debt grew, but none of the money left New York, where it lingered to pay interest to **U.S creditors holding the bonds.**" The world's debt is estimated at $37 trillion. At just 10% interest, there is no way to pay it off.

Now add to this the normal human feelings of jealousy, selfishness and greed and you have the makings for hatred of the "haves" by the "have-nots." It is not just the Muslims that feel that we are keeping them down. The Chinese, Koreans, Russians, Africans, and Central and South America all feel that we intend to keep them down. Now mix the enemy of all mankind into this and you have the makings of a world war against America.

Right now, the world needs America. But if America were to collapse economically, the world would not care. Their many merchants would miss us, but the average citizen would be jumping for joy. On 9-11, much of the Muslim community rejoiced at the thought that someone had brought America down. It didn't last of course, but it did show how they feel about the U.S.

Politicians will be as bewildered as anybody. In Israel today the people want peace so bad that a leading politician has said that they would make a deal with the devil, if it meant peace. Israel needs the United States, but God will make them willing to rely on Him. The way He will do that is to take away their leaning post and He will do that thru a massive earthquake.

It will be a cataclysmic upheaval that will destroy the financial integrity of most if not all western capitalist societies. Such an earthquake would render the <u>United States impotent in a matter of minutes.</u> Unstoppable fires will rage and no one will have the water to put them out even if the roads were passable.

Now I want to be clear, **I love the United States and I am very thankful to be an American Citizen.** Anyone who doesn't love the USA should have to live overseas for a while. Even the so-called advanced nations of Europe are behind the USA in standard of living. Americans have a lot to be thankful for. But the America that used to exist is now only a memory.

A selfish spoiled people have replaced the great generation that defeated Hitler. Given the open hostility that exists in politics and lack of civility, it's a wonder anything ever gets done in Washington.

There would be no way to rebuild given our current debt load. Our main concern that day would be survival. Foreign affairs would be left to others; the nation will be in a fight to survive.

One hurricane was more than our government could handle. What will it do if the New Madrid fault were to erupt in a **magnitude 8 quake?** That alone would cause billions of dollars in damage. What would happen if it came in mid winter? Some of the <u>largest gas lines</u> in America come right across the fault zone.

What would happen to the heat for the **northeast?** Their natural gas would not get there. How would those people react? What about **St. Louis** and **Memphis?** Those cities are old and the infrastructure is failing now. What happens when the ground begins to shake?

If the government couldn't get food to New Orleans quickly enough, then how are they going to feed the inner cities? America is not ready to meet its judgment. Yet judgment is coming just the same.

Quite simply, there will be wide spread **panic, riots** and **chaos** in the streets of America. People down thru history behave the same when they are scared and hungry. Instinct for survival is priority number one, and God help anyone or anything that gets in their way.

The need for food will outweigh the need for peace. Men and women will sell all that they own to have a scrap of food. Like Esau of old, people will gladly sell out for their bellies. I firmly believe that the mentality that exists today where someone can get killed for simply looking at somebody wrong is not conducive to surviving anything.

Let me be crystal clear, I'm only talking about one earthquake. The bible talks about a monstrous quake that will shake the entire world! We can not sustain one medium size quake, how can we hope to survive a big one?

I am not trying to be a fear-monger. What I am trying to do is wake up a sleeping church and an apathetic world. **<u>Christ is coming back</u>**! And when He returns for His bride the church, trouble like this world has never imagined will be unleashed.

Governments are going to fall. People will have no way to get food or water or medicines. People's hearts will fail them for fear. There will be no peace to the world that has rejected the Prince of Peace.

Since the great Christmas quake of 2004 scientist have been watching the recent earthquakes and volcanic eruptions closely. They've found that from 2002 to 2005 underwater earthquakes and volcanic eruptions have **increased by a staggering 88%. Continental quakes have increased by over 60%!**

The three largest earthquakes recorded in the last two hundred years occurred in a three month period!

Something is happening. The earthquakes are getting more numerous and are becoming more powerful.

The Christmas earthquake that caused the tsunami was estimated to be **9.2**. It rocked the earth (**Isaiah 24:19-20** [19] (GW) *The earth will be completely broken. The earth will shake back and forth violently. The earth will stagger.* [20] *the earth will stumble like a drunk and sway like a shack in the wind.*), causing the planet to wobble momentarily. We also lost about two seconds of time, due to the planet basically stalling in space due to the quake. According to the bible, a far more severe quake is coming!

1Thessalonians 5:3. *For when they shall say Peace and Safety,* ***sudden destruction.*** *Again I want to remind you, God wants us to warn the world. It is going to be "sudden" and it is going to be "destruction". We are going to answer for not warning people. If we really believe God then we must relay His word to the world.*

A Partial List Of Recent Earthquakes Around The World.

End Times - 21st century Earthquakes

January 26, 2001 – India; A earthquake measuring 7.7 struck the western state of Gujarat and neighboring Pakistan, killing at least 19,700 people.

March 26, 2002 – Afghanistan; At least 1,800 people were killed when a series of earthquakes struck northern Afghanistan and destroyed the district capital of Nahrin.

June 22, 2002 – Iran; A quake measuring a 6 killed at least 500 people in northwestern Iran.

February 24, 2003 – China; A 6.3 earthquake killed at least 266 people in western China.

May 1, 2003 – Turkey; A 6.4 quake killed 167 people in southwestern Turkey.

December 26, 2003 – Iran; A massive earthquake killed more than 30,000 people in Bam, Iran.

December 26, 2004 –Northern Sumatra– A 9.0 underwater earthquake devastated the Indian Ocean region with tsunamis that killed over 283,000 people.

October 8, 2005 – Kashmir; A 7.6-7.8 earthquake killed between 100,000 and 150,000 people. Many more people are still homeless.

May 26, 2006 – Java, Indonesia; A 6.3 earthquake killed over 6,000 people and seriously injured another 33,000. More than 200,000 are homeless.

At the moment of the Rapture of the Church, there will be a massive worldwide earthquake. Many people will die and national infrastructure will be destroyed.

Sadly most of the world's population is centered along coastal areas. As we saw from the tsunami in 2004, many people will perish from the flood waters. Literally millions of people will die in a matter of hours.

The chance of survival will depend on whether or not the ground or building that was holding someone up was solid enough. If the San Andreas Fault erupted in a major quake, most of San Francisco and Los Angeles would be destroyed. Fire alone would destroy many city blocks and neighborhoods. If it got into the nearby hills, it could spread unchecked over thousands of miles.

Many of the areas at risk are along the Ring of Fire and are largely populated. The ring of fire is the area along the Pacific Ocean which is ringed with volcanoes and fault lines. Major earthquakes hitting those areas today could produce terrible damage. Most global cities have at least tripled their populations in the last hundred years, so a major earthquake would collapse virtually all infrastructures.

Millions of people could feel the shock waves, not only of the initial tremor, but of the aftershocks, landslides, floods, and raging fires. That's not even taking into effect the fact that airports would be destroyed also. Earthquakes can trigger landslides, tsunamis, avalanches, and cause flooding as dams break. California mudslides also would occur. Without passable highways and the bridges knocked out there will be almost no way to get aid to those who need it. FEMA will be powerless to help.

<u>Unlike many popular teachings there is no proof in scripture that the world will wake up and go looking for us.</u> Neither is there any

proof that all the babies will be missing. <u>Neither Noah nor Lot took the babies</u> with them to escape the destruction to come. I know this goes against conventional teaching, but it is in line with scripture. **If you want to make sure your children go to heaven, you and you alone are responsible**. Do not count on God taking them and leaving you! **You be ready and get them ready, it's your child and your responsibility!**

According to **1Corinthians 7:14,** the believer sanctifies their children and their families. It never says that the unbeliever sanctifies their children. Mister or lady, if you don't want your children or grandchildren going thru the tribulation then please get saved and pray over them.

All over the earth people will be panicking and scrambling for survival. One thing that is obvious after watching the devastation of New Orleans is that sinners only look after themselves.

What will happen when only sinners are left? The United States is already several trillion dollars in debt. How could we handle a major nation wide catastrophe? I believe the reason the U.S is only alluded to in Scripture is because it will be digging out and unable to impact the world any longer. Understand this; hungry people will absolutely do anything to fill their stomach.

If they have to kill, they will. When all the welfare is gone and the store shelves are empty, where will the people go for food? They will go to the country and the farmers land.

Can this happen in America? Yes, it can and I believe in the tribulation it will.

Where is the U.S in prophecy? It has fallen.

Let me be clear, the United States is going to fall. I believe that a massive earthquake will take it out. Israel will be forced to defend itself without our help. Why is God going to allow the U.S to be brought down?

Consider these facts; we send more porn overseas than anyone else. We have aborted over 40 million babies since 1973. We have allowed the A.C.L.U to take God out of American life.

We have promoted the homosexual cause <u>to our children</u>. We allow Islam to be promoted in our colleges, **yet throw out Christianity**. We have spent ourselves into a nine trillion dollar debt. And worse of all, we are **turning our backs on Israel,** the one nation that God chose over all others.

I don't believe that given our welfare mentality we can cope with doing without anything for long. Americans are too used to having everything they want in life. **We value our wants over our needs.** When the government even hints at taking away some of our entitlements the protest are very loud and sometimes violent.

We expect our government to take care of our **<u>WANTS.</u>** We are Americans; **we don't have to do without.** Even our poor live better than most other people on Earth. We now have more overweight people in America than we do skinny. How poor are our people when the number one health issue is obesity?

Let a natural disaster hit and the number one response of the people and politicians alike are to blame someone. We have lost our moral compass. We don't want to make tough decisions. We don't want to pay the consequences of our actions. We only want to have a good time. In short, we are setting ourselves up for a fall.

One more very important thing to take note of, after the rapture, **<u>the praying church is gone</u>**. The one thing that people in New Orleans could count on wasn't the government; **it was the church that responded**. The prayers of the church hold back the power of the devil. Our prayers help the needy and the sick. Our prayers bring deliverance to the captives.

Once the prayers of the church are gone, this world will not be able to withstand the onslaught of the devil. People who think that they can get saved during the tribulation period are in for a tremendous shock! **<u>The very fact that they even think about getting saved is because some one is praying for them.</u>** Without somebody praying, many people would be so tormented by the devil that even sleep would be impossible.

Another thing to consider, the world hates the U.S.A. It is not going to come to our aid. God is aligning the world for the final showdown. The devil is not now nor has he ever been in control of the situations on earth, God is in control.

This is why the world is coming to hate the U.S. They are doing what God has allowed them to do. The devil hates us because we are the primary source of the Gospel being spread across the world. God just allowed him to spread that hatred around to serve God's purpose.

Why does the Muslim world hate the US and Israel?

For one thing, we give Israel over $3 Billion dollars annually. The Muslims see this as being pro-Israeli, which it is. Israel is the only real democracy in the Middle East and therefore it is thriving! The Arabs hate Israel because of their success and wealth and because the devil hates Israel. It is the devil that drives them to hate, God never tells us to hate our enemies, but to love our enemies. Israel with 6 million people has a 100 billion dollar economy. That's better than Russia with 150 million people. The Arabs' hate and envy Israel. Instead of being ashamed that they haven't even come close to Israel's success, they blame Israel for their own incompetence.

What would make a young mother strap bombs around her waist and blow herself up? Hate. What would make a child shout out how he wants to kill all Jews? Hate. Only Islam preaches and practices hate as a way of life. Jesus said we should love our enemies and do good to those who would despitefully use us.

Islam teaches its adherents to kill, terrorize and torment its adversaries at every opportunity. How can such a people ever learn to love? Only thru Jesus.

Arab ego is very fragile; they see themselves as having been humiliated by the west. Remember these are people who still kill each other over things that happened over 1,000 years ago. They don't forget many wrongs. Killing for alleged wrongs are common in Muslim society.

The church on earth after the rapture.

Without sounding too judgmental I think it is safe to say that there will be many churches in which no one will be raptured. This is because their pastors have taught them that being members and shaking the preachers hand was everything that God required of them. There is not a desire to follow the Lord Jesus' example or to get close to God. They consider themselves Christian, but couldn't begin to defend the Christian faith. In short, they are only church going sinners.

I don't blame them as much as I blame the organizations that teach such damnable heresy. Their teaching has allowed people to commit grievous sins without guilt. When the apostle Paul warned the churches "to awake to righteousness and sin not" it wasn't a request, it was a command. God said to "be holy for I am holy". Was He asking or ordering?

After the rapture, those who know what has happened will need to do two things fast. **Number one** is to repent. Don't say that you are sorry unless you are willing to die for it; because in all probability you will. True repentance is a <u>turning around</u> and a <u>dropping of anything</u> that does not please God.

Number two is to grab a Bible and study to show yourself approved unto God. Get His word in you as fast as you can. Only by knowing God and His word and keeping your prayer life fresh, can you withstand in the evil day. **You may have to give your life for Jesus, but you at least will be saved.**

Chapter seven: the redeemed.

As soon as the rapture takes place the wind stops blowing. Not one tree feels the breeze. There is no way of knowing how long this last, but the spiritual significance is great. Once the church is gone, the wind of the Holy Spirit Revival as we have known it will stop blowing. The next revival will be by choice of beheading for Jesus, not merely walking down the isle to the altar.

There is something here we need to focus our attention on. The four angels that are bound in the Euphrates River in chapter **9:13-19** are prepared for a specific time to kill one-third of mankind. I believe that chapter seven is speaking of the same angels. They are obviously fallen angels because their role is to hurt the earth and the sea. God uses them to achieve judgment on the people of this world.

The 144,000 sealed Israelites.

We are told that these are out of each tribe, or that they are a representative of each tribe. 12,000 per tribe times twelve equals 144,000. The Islamic teaching that I find interesting here is that the prophets in Jerusalem develop a following of Jewish men and women. We of course don't base our teachings on what they have to say except to show that the devil also has a plan to deceive by stating a lie before the fact.

According to the teachings of Islam, these Jews convert to follow the prophet in Jerusalem. I think it's safe to say that the enemy is already at work trying to convince his followers to not believe their testimony.

I personally believe that the 144,000 will be

Jewish converts to Christianity. The testimony of Elijah and Enoch will cause many to believe in Jesus. They will be killed along with the two witnesses by the antichrist. It is clear that these people are on the earth at the time that they are sealed for the angel says to the four fallen angels to not hurt the earth or the sea.

Moslems also have expectations of an antichrist; they call him al-Masih al-Dajjal ("Messiah-Liar"). He will (according to them) **deify Christ** and pervert the **words of the true Messiah**. He will appear towards the end of this civilization. The location is variously given **as the Jewish** quarter.

The Muslims will hate the prophet in Jerusalem because he will "**deify Jesus Christ**". That is, he will say <u>Jesus is Gods Son</u>. The Muslims also will not accept his teaching from the Bible concerning Jesus. I think this proves that the devil knows that Elijah will **preach Jesus** during the tribulation period. That's why he is at work to dispute the validity of the Bible.

The idea of <u>deifying Jesus</u> is upsetting to Muslims because their prophet claimed to know **for a fact** <u>from God Himself that Jesus was not the Son of God, and that He was never crucified.</u>

"Far be it from His [Allah's] glory that He should have a son!"— The Koran, Sura IV

A true Christian is not upset in the least when someone attacks his beliefs. After all, if the Word of God is what they are attacking then it is in reality God who will defend the Word. It isn't up to me to prove God. I just trust Him and know that in the end God will prove to the world Who He is.

The False Gospel that Muslims love; the gospel of Barnabas, circa 1,400 AD. The following is an excerpt from the bogus gospel.

When the soldiers with Judas drew near to the place where Jesus was, Jesus heard the approach of many people, wherefore in <u>fear he withdrew</u> (**he ran like a scared rabbit**) <u>into the house.</u>

And the eleven were sleeping (**there is no mention here of the garden of Gethsemane**).

Then God, seeing the <u>danger of his servant,</u> (**apparently God had just noticed what was going on**) commanded Gabriel, Michael, Rafael, and Uriel, his ministers, to take <u>Jesus out of the world. The holy angels came and **took Jesus out** by the window that looks toward the South; they bare him and placed him in the third heaven in the company of angels blessing God for evermore.</u>

(The next part has Judas being tried in Jesus' place, though no one seems to know that it is Judas. They think it is Jesus lying to them.)

Judas answered: 'I have told you that I am Judas Iscariot, who promised to give into your hands Jesus the Nazarene; and you, by what are I know not, are beside yourselves, for you will have it by every means that I am Jesus.'

The high priest answered: 'O perverse seducer, you have deceived all Israel, beginning from Galilee; even to Jerusalem here, with your doctrine and false miracles: and now think you to flee the merited punishment that befits you by feigning to be mad?

<u>Here is the lie that is told</u> that Jesus was translated and that Judas was crucified in His place. It is beyond absurd to think that all the eyewitnesses who watched Jesus for over three years as well as His mother and His brothers could not figure out who He was! The disciples recognized Judas instantly when he came with the soldiers. At least two of Jesus' half brothers died for the faith. Of all the people who said that they saw Jesus raised from the dead after He was killed, **over 500 at one time**, not one retracted his story later. And remember, most gave their lives to prove their faith!

Muhammad said that God deceived the Jews and fooled Jesus' followers. Sounds like a lie doesn't it? How could a **God that can not lie** do such a thing? Quite simply He could not. But the father of lies sure could. You see, if God lied, He would be a son of the devil. Jesus said the devil was the father of lies. It originated with the devil, not God. For God to take on the devils characteristics would put the devil above God.

Everything that Muhammad taught was contingent on these lies; that Jesus was never crucified, that He did not die for anyone's sins, and that He never claimed to be Gods' Son. If Muslims would accept the historical evidence of the crucifixion, which is abundant, then they could see what a trick of the devil these lies are.

Why would God have tricked every single first century believer? What kind of God would perpetrate a lie in the first place? Why would God allow these men and women to go into the world preaching something that He did not believe Himself? Remember there are over 5,000 manuscripts and fragments that back up the Christian position and faith. What kind of God would allow these to survive but not allow any of His views to survive from the first century of the Christian church? Surely even the Muslims must believe that God is more powerful than the devil. Surely God could have saved His word for us to study. Well, He did and we still have it, it's called the Bible.

Rev. 7:1-4

After this I saw four angels standing at the four corners of the earth. They were holding back the four winds of the earth to keep them from blowing on the land, the sea, or any tree. ²I saw another angel coming from the east with the seal of the living God. He cried out in a loud voice to the four angels who had been allowed to harm the land and sea, ³"Don't harm the land, the sea, or the trees until we have put the seal on the foreheads of the servants of our God."
⁴I heard how many were sealed: 144,000. Those who were sealed were from every tribe of the people of Israel:

The angels can not harm the land or sea or any trees, which proves that they are on the earth. It is on the earth that the 144,000 are sealed. Unlike the innumerable host that John saw in Heaven, these are still here on earth.

In **chapter 14:3,** John tells us the definition of who they are. Verse four says, "These are pure virgins, they are followers **of the Lamb,** they have been redeemed", which in the Greek means purchased, and they sing a song no one else could sing.

I will have more to say concerning the last revival on Earth during the Tribulation Period when we get to chapter 11.

Chapter six

The Tribulation Period Begins When The Seventh Seal Is Broken

The Seventh Seal; The Tribulation Begins

Revelation ch.8:1

1 (GW) **When he opened the seventh seal, there was silence in heaven for about half an hour.**

The title of the book is the **Revealing of Jesus Christ**. Here we have the full revelation of Jesus and heaven stops for about half an hour at the sight. The purpose of the book is to reveal Jesus. This is accomplished by the subjugation of all opposition to His kingdom, **1Cor. 15:25.**

JESUS, NAME ABOVE ALL NAMES, KING OF KINGS AND LORD OF LORDS, begins now to exert full control over the earth and to put down rebellion and to defend Israel.

Notice the first thing that happens once the church is out of the earth, judgment is not promised any longer, it is delivered!

After heaven has stood silent for half an hour, the prayers of the saints break the silence. Prayers, long and short, joyful and sorrowful, yet all are powerful! Now it is prayers of imperfect men and women that break the silence in the Holy of Holies!

Everything up to now has been a mere prelude to the actual tribulation. The antichrist is loosed before this, but he can not conquer until that which hinders is taken out of the way according to **2 Thessalonians 2:7-8.**

Many have said that the Holy Spirit is that which hinders so therefore He will leave the earth at the time of the rapture. According to **David in Psalms 139**, there is no place in heaven or hell that we can go to escape His presence. To say the Spirit will leave the earth is unscriptural.

What then is **"that which hinders"?** There are two viable possibilities, one would be the church. The church has probably never realized just how powerful its prayers are. If it is the church withholding the antichrist, then our prayers are the only thing stopping the manifestation of the antichrist today. He can't take over **until we stop praying**. And we will not stop praying until we are "taken out of the way"!

The other possibility is that "he which hinders" is Elijah the prophet who will minister for 3.5 years before being killed by the antichrist. There is a definite logic to that argument. Until the two witnesses are killed, the beast can't set himself in the temple of God, showing himself to be God. So Elijah could well be the hindering one.

Look at verse one. At the opening of the book in chapter eight, heaven falls silent. Now something tremendous happens, prayers of all the saints are offered up to God!

See the picture God gives us; the church is gone from the earth, but the very thing that shakes the earth once we are gone is the prayers we prayed while here! Even though we are gone, we still have power in our prayers and they are neither forgotten nor silent. They still move Heaven and Earth! Wow!

The tribulation begins!
The Seven Trumpets, ch.8:6-13, 9:1-21

Revelation 8:6-13

6 (GW) The seven angels who had the seven trumpets got ready to blow them.
7 When the first angel blew his trumpet, hail and fire were mixed with blood, and were thrown on the earth. One-third of the earth was burned up, one-third of the trees were burned up, and all the green grass was burned up.

The first trumpet; one third of vegetation is destroyed. For those who think that they can somehow survive the tribulation period by living off the land, God has an answer, NO YOU CAN'T! One third of all vegetation wiped out will mean even worse famine than before. What would happen if the food supply were destroyed by one third?

There is an example of this happening in history. **The Great Famine of 1315-1317** in northern Europe caused millions of deaths. Bad weather in the spring of 1315 caused crop failures that lasted thru the summer of 1317.

It was a period **marked by extreme levels of criminal activity** as people did anything they could to survive. **It was also marked by high levels of disease and mass deaths, cannibalism and infanticide.** With the grass gone, the cattle will starve. Without the cattle, people will starve. The entire food chain will shut down overnight.

The Second Trumpet; The Sea Is Polluted

⁸ When the second angel blew his trumpet, something like a huge mountain burning with fire was thrown into the sea. One-third of the sea turned into blood,
⁹ one-third of the creatures that were living in the sea died, and one-third of the ships were destroyed.

The second trumpet; one third of all life in the waters dies; many ships are destroyed. Now what hope people may have had of survival is dashed, only the ocean can offer hope to a starving world and it is polluted. The result of the oceans being polluted would be catastrophic.

Many have speculated on this being a meteor or comet crashing into the ocean. Whatever it is, we can be sure that it will result in much misery on the planet.

Already today drinkable water is becoming harder to come by. The United States has been blessed to have so much fresh water. In much of the world the people drink unclean water laced with viruses and pollutants. Infant mortality is extremely high already due to the bad water. In the tribulation fresh water will be worth more than gold or silver or even oil.

All of the fisheries along our coast will be out of work. Many people's livelihood will be gone. How will they hope to survive? Already fishermen around the world are over fishing the oceans. Starvation on an unbelievable scale is coming.

The Third Trumpet; The Fresh Water Is Polluted

¹⁰ When the third angel blew his trumpet, a huge star flaming like a torch fell from the sky. It fell on one-third of the rivers and on the springs.
¹¹ That star was named Wormwood. One-third of the water turned into wormwood, and many people died from this water because it had turned bitter.

The third trumpet; one third of all drinkable water is made poisonous. Many will die from the poison water. From the picture it seems obvious that a meteorite or some such occurrence is the cause of the poisoning of the waters. All water originates in the ocean. Evaporation gives us rain which in turn filters into the soil and gives us fresh drinking water. If the ocean is severely polluted then even evaporation would not cleanse it. The result would be poisonous drinking water.

An interesting fact; wormwood in Russian is Chernobyl, as in the nuclear reactor that imploded on itself.

The wormwood plant is extremely bitter and hard to digest, usually making the persons stomach very upset. The meaning of the name is clear. John wants us to get the picture; to drink the water will make you sick to your stomach. Even so people will drink it. They have to in order to survive.

The Fourth Trumpet; Darkness Fills The Sky

¹² When the fourth angel blew his trumpet, one-third of the sun, one-third of the moon, and one-third of the stars were struck so that one-third of them turned dark. There was no light for one-third of the day and one-third of the night.
¹³ I saw an eagle flying overhead, and I heard it say in a loud voice, "Catastrophe, catastrophe, catastrophe for those living on earth, because of the remaining trumpet blasts which the three angels are about to blow."

I have no doubt that this means that smoke will cover the atmosphere to such an extent that even at noon it will seem like twilight. The smoke will probably be the result of the fires that will be burning from the star that falls upon the earth polluting the waters. Also volcanic eruptions can send thousands of tons of dust into the sky. There have been several documented cases of that dust changing the earth's weather patterns resulting in drought in one place and cold, wet summers in another.

The effect of the sun being blocked from view may well be that the Ultra-Violet Radiation will actually increase on earth. This would mean an increase in non melanoma skin cancer. If the smoke and gasses increased in the upper atmosphere it would cause the earth to warm up considerably. This would kill off many plants and animals.

The Fifth Trumpet; Smoke And Locust

Rev. 9:1-3

The fifth angel sounded his trumpet, and I saw a star that had fallen from the sky to the earth. The star was given the key to the shaft of the Abyss. ²When he opened the Abyss, smoke rose from it like the smoke from a gigantic furnace. The sun and sky were darkened by the smoke from the Abyss. ³And out of the smoke locusts came down upon the earth and were given power like that of scorpions of the earth.

From John's description it is evident that these are spiritual creatures. There is no doubt that their stings will literally torment men, causing them much pain, but they are indeed spiritual in nature. For an understanding of this consider the Egyptians. When they resisted God thru Moses, God who is a Spirit struck them with boils. The plague started in the Spirit, but was felt in the flesh.

That is what is happening here. For further proof that they are spiritual look at <u>verse 11, they have a king, which is the angel of the bottomless pit.</u> Also, they are described in such a way that is clearly seen to be spiritual. There is nothing in their description that would lead you to believe otherwise.

*³And out of the smoke locusts **came down** upon the earth.* Literally there will fall from the polluted sky a skin disease that will cause severe burning and boils. This is similar to what happened to the Egyptians thru Moses and Aaron. Once again I want to emphasize that these are spiritual locust but they are manifesting in the natural. Sin affects your spirit and your flesh.

THE LOCUST

Rev. 9:5-6

*They were not given power to kill them, but only to **torture them for five months**. And the agony they suffered was like that of the sting of a scorpion when it strikes a man. 6**During those days men will seek death, but will not find it; they will long to die, but death will elude them.***
What a horrible state to be in, to desire to die and be unable to. If anything would make you want to get saved and stay saved that should do it. This will be a five months long plague that will sting and burn but people will not die from it, though they surely want to.

The sting of a scorpion causes immediate pain and burning but very little swelling. The area becomes very sensitive to the touch as well as having numbness and a tingling feeling. The black scorpion is probably the worse. It can make the persons face to go numb, give them blurry vision and muscle twitching. Some times hyperactivity and uncontrollable eye movements also accompany the other symptoms.

They are given power to torment the people for five months. This means that one sting or outbreak will cause symptoms that last for five months. **What a horrible time to be an unbeliever!** People may ridicule Christians, but they forget that we actually know what is coming! We are not the crazy ones; they are for allowing themselves to go thru the tribulation.

The Sixth Trumpet; Demonic Army Is Loosed To Kill One-third Of Men

Rev. 9:13-21

*The sixth angel sounded his trumpet, and I heard a voice coming from the horns of the golden altar that is before God. 14It said to the sixth angel who had the trumpet, "Release the four angels who are bound at the great river Euphrates." 15And the four angels who had been kept ready for this very hour and day and month and year were released to kill a third of mankind. 16**The number of the mounted troops was two hundred million. I heard their number.***

17 The horses and riders I saw in my vision looked like this: Their breastplates were fiery red, dark blue, and yellow as sulfur. The heads of the horses resembled the heads of lions, and out of their mouths came fire, smoke and sulfur. ***18 A third of mankind was killed by the three plagues of fire, smoke and sulfur that came out of their mouths.*** *19 The power of the horses was in their mouths and in their tails; for their tails were like snakes, having heads with which they inflict injury.*

The four angels are bound, which is clear evidence that these are **fallen angels**. They are prepared for this very hour to kill the **third part of men**. Many try to make the scripture say something that it doesn't say here. It is clear that the description is not of men and helicopters or tanks, but of **spiritual beings. 200 million loosed upon mankind to kill!**

The Chinese army may number over 200 million, but so does the united Arab armies. These creatures kill one third of mankind long before the battle of Armageddon. That would mean a nation of people was out destroying other nations for no apparent reason. No these are definitely spiritual beings.

Men Refuse To Acknowledge God And Repent

*20 The rest of mankind that were not killed by these plagues still **did not repent** of the work of their hands; they **did not stop worshiping demons,** and idols of gold, silver, bronze, stone and wood--idols that cannot see or hear or walk. 21 Nor did they repent of their murders, their magic arts, their sexual immorality or their thefts.*

THINGS THEY DID NOT REPENT OF;

1. **The works of their hands.** Darwinism teaches that we are all there is. The fittest must advance even at the cost of destroying the weak. Human evolution is a belief system. To have faith in a theory that disputes the existence or need for God puts you at war with God. It makes you God. There are no self made men in Heaven. In case you think that Jesus was self made, consider this fact; over 40 times in the Gospel of John Jesus said He came because the Father sent Him. Never one time did Jesus claim to do His own will. The only will that mattered to Jesus was the Fathers will. No He most certainly

was not self made, He was God made! **Acts 10:38.** Idolatry includes worship of self.

2. **The worship of demons.** The Apostle Paul told the Corinthian church that what the pagans worshipped was demons, even if they did not know it. There can be no doubt that Hinduism, Buddhism as well as many other religions all worship demons. When they invoke a spirit to repel a sickness or bad karma, they are dealing with demon spirits. Amazingly many so-called educated Americans give credence to these teachings. They worship demons and don't even know it.

3. **Murders.** There are many reasons why people will be committing murders during the tribulation. Hunger, hate, revenge and fear can all be dangerous tools in the devils hands. Killing in the name of religion is also of the devil. For whatever reason there may be, the people will not be able to understand that repentance is their only hope.

4. **SORCERIES-PHARMAKIA.** Most drugs in John's time had only one use; to cause the user to see visions and aid in whatever worship he was involved in. Today the word has a far different meaning. Pharmacia in today's vocabulary means drugs, pure and simple. Yet in reality the meaning is still the same. Many people use drugs, legal and illegal, to stimulate their lives even at the cost of their families, jobs, and health. Can that not be said to be worship? It is demonic and **it is not Godly to abuse drugs, no matter who uses them.**

5. **FORNIFICATION.** Here is a definition of the word translated fornication in the Greek; porneia

Thayer Definition:

1) Illicit sexual intercourse
A) Adultery, fornication, homosexuality, lesbianism, intercourse with animals etc.
B) Sexual intercourse with close relatives; Lev. 18

So we see that any perverted sexual behavior is considered sin. This is talking about sex outside the marriage covenant, homosexuality and all forms of perversion. The porn industry sells billions worldwide. There is a definite demand for the product or it would not sell. God demands repentance as a condition for salvation. Men will not repent and give up this idolatry either.

7. **THEFTS.** This word means not just stealing, but the act of stealing, hiding what is stolen, and condoning stealing. During the tribulation there will be much crime, way more than has ever been. Many people will steal in order to have food. But as we saw in New Orleans, many steal because they like to steal.

During the New York City blackout, rapes, robberies and murders increased dramatically. Why? Because those people who did the acts felt that they could get away with it.

We are now two generations removed from having prayer in our public schools. What has been the net result? A harder, meaner generation has grown up. They think nothing of human life. We allowed the schools to tell them that they are only intelligent primates. By the time they have reached adulthood they will have seen countless murders on Television. They lack a moral center.

One more point about the plague; it killed men by these three things.

1. fire
2. smoke
3. sulfur

None of these things are spiritual and none of them come from insects or any other creature. What they represent is God using natural things as punishment on rebellious men. A volcano puts out fire, smoke and sulfur. This sounds very much like a series of volcanic eruptions which will bring devastation to much of the world. The resultant smoke from the volcanoes will block out the sun and change weather patterns across the globe. **One third of mankind would mean an additional two billion more people killed.**

Chapter seven

The seventh trumpet; all kingdoms are now Christ'

Rev. 11:14-19

The second woe has passed; the third woe is coming soon.

15The seventh angel sounded his trumpet, and there were loud voices in heaven, which said: "The kingdom of the world has become the kingdom of our Lord and of his Christ, and he will reign for ever and ever."

*16And the twenty-four elders, who were seated on their thrones before God, fell on their faces and worshiped God, 17saying: "We give thanks to you, Lord God Almighty, the One who is and who was, **because you have taken your great power and have begun to reign.***

18The nations were angry; and your wrath has come.

The time has come for judging the dead,

and for rewarding your servants the prophets

and your saints and those who reverence your name,

both small and great--and for destroying those who destroy the earth."

19Then God's temple in heaven was opened, and within his temple was seen the ark of his covenant. And there came flashes of lightning, rumblings, and peals of thunder, an earthquake and a great hailstorm.

He will destroy those who have destroyed the earth. At the risk of sounding like a tree hugging environmentalist, I want to say that the ones who destroy this earth either by polluting or wiping out whole tracts of rain forest are going to answer for it. Christians should be the best stewards of the land that there are. There is no excuse for destroying this good earth that God put into our hands. God takes this seriously.

The Temple in Heaven is open again and the Ark of the Covenant is seen in it. Notice that it says that the temple is open **AGAIN.** For a while it had been closed. This coincides with Jesus taking the power and the kingdom as He begins to reign.

<u>**VS. 17;**</u>

"We give thanks to you, Lord God Almighty;
The One who is and who was, **because you have taken your great power**
and <u>**have begun to reign.**</u>

The importance here is sometimes lost on us. Christ takes ownership of this world and its possessions. The obvious questions arise, were not all these things already His? Indeed they are, but at this present hour they are in the hands of the world system.

<u>*Hebrews 2:8*</u>

You have put all things in subjection under his feet.
For in that He put all in subjection under him, He left nothing that is not put under him. **But now we do not yet see all things put under him.**

But here the news is broadcast from heaven to the earth; the kingdoms of the world are **NOW BECOME** the kingdoms of our Lord and of His Christ! Jesus told of the man who planted a vineyard and lent it out to other men. When the time came for Him to receive fruit they sent His servants away empty and killed some. After a while He sent His Son. They also killed Him. What did He do then? He came and killed those men. Jesus was speaking of the Jews in this parable but it also applies to all men. By rejecting Him, you bring judgment on yourself. He will claim what is rightfully His.

Between the <u>sixth and seventh trumpets</u> there is a pause. In **chapter 10**, John sees the angel who has a little book who stands upon the land and sea. This makes it clear that ownership of the earth has no limits to Jesus; He is the Lord of land and sea.

<u>This angel proclaims that *"there shall be DELAY no more"* and that *"the mystery* (the church, **Rom. 16:25; Col. 1:25-27; Eph. 3:1-7**.)</u> Here there is a need to establish what God is speaking about. The church age is called a **mystery** by the Apostle Paul because Jewish teachers never saw it coming though it was in the prophets and Moses that God would raise up the Gentiles to provoke the Jews to jealousy. Jesus first used the word **mystery** in connection with the kingdom of God in **Mark 4:11.**

The other places where it is used of Jesus or the church are; **Romans 11:25, 1Cor.2:7, 1Cor. 15:51, Eph 1:9, 3:3,3:4, 3:9,5:32, 6:19, Col.1:26,1:27,2:2,4:3, 1Timothy 3:9,3:16, Rev.1:20, 10:7.**

The word "mystery" is used of the spirit of antichrist in **2Thessalonians 2:7** where Paul calls it the mystery of lawlessness. Here he is clearly referring to a man and a religious system. Note the harmony with Gods' definition of Ishmael in **Genesis 16:12** *and he shall be as a wild donkey among men; his hand shall be against every man, and every man's hand against him.* This same lawlessness is seen today in Islam. They literally are against every man and every man has been forced to be against them.

This is the spirit of lawlessness that will rule in the last days thru the antichrist. Lawlessness does not mean without law but instead means one who does not recognize the legitimate law. The antichrist does not recognize Gods' covenant with the nation of Israel and the land of Canaan. He is Muslim and they refuse to accept the fact that Israel has any claim to the land.

In Revelation 17:5&7 the religious system is called a Mystery. This word is always used to signify that something is religious. **Chapter 10:7; *the Mystery of God shall be finished".*** As opposed to the "mystery of satan" which also will be finished but not for its glory as it will be destroyed.

This verse has confused people for years because many insist on reading the book in a chronological manner. It is clear that what God is doing here is that He is going back to something that has been covered already one way, and explaining it in more detail.

I believe that the day of the **SEVENTH TRUMPET** will literally be the end, that's what the bible says **(verse 7).** From this point on though there is an exit out of the Holiest. Grasp this truth, thru Christ we can go in and out, but now God allows every believer to experience His presence where they are. As Christ is shown to now be reigning, access is also shown. There is a direct correlation to Ezekiel's experience with the book in Ezekiel 3. He also ate the book with the same results. The book of Ezekiel is drawn upon considerably.

The Tribulation Temple

Rev. 11:1-12
Then I was given a reed like a measuring rod. And the angel stood, saying, "Rise and measure the temple of God, the altar, and those who worship there. ²But leave out the court which is outside the temple, and do not measure it, for it has been given to the Gentiles. And they will tread the holy city underfoot for forty-two months (**3.5 years**).

Although the Gentiles will tread the Temple Mount under foot for 3.5 years, **it will be the last half of the tribulation period, not the first half**. This speaks of what will happen after the antichrist kills the two witnesses. John, like Ezekiel before him, measured the temple. The measurements are not given by John.

What God is showing us is the temple that will be rebuilt- the third temple of the Nation of Israel. The Al-Aqsa mosque will be destroyed at the beginning of the tribulation, whether by earthquake or by the two witnesses.

Right now there are actually three mosques on the temple compound. One is underground and two are on the top of the mount area. God is going to allow them to be removed from His holy site. There will be a new temple built on Mt. Moriah, the site of the original one built by Solomon and sanctified by God.

God's presence came down upon the first temple when it was dedicated. The ground is not just sacred to the Jews, it is sanctified to God. He was there! It is His place and no one should even think about stopping Israel from rebuilding His house. It is the temple mount that is the center of the universe as far as God is concerned. The Jews believe that in order for the Messiah to come they must first build His temple.

In Ezra's day God sent two prophets to Jerusalem to help him and Nehemiah build the second temple. Those two men were Zechariah and Haggai. They were used of God to rally the people and the leaders to build and the temple would probably have not been built except for their ministries. That is exactly how it will be during the ministries of Enoch and Elijah.

The Gentiles will tread the outer court under foot for 3.5 years. This signifies the fact that the last half of the tribulation will be when the antichrist is actually able to put a stop to temple worship.

The Two Witnesses In Jerusalem Enoch And Elijah

Rev 10:3: *And I will give power to my two witnesses, and they will prophesy one thousand two hundred and sixty days* (3.5 years), *clothed in sackcloth."* *⁴These are the two olive trees and the two lamp stands standing before the God of the earth.* (Zec. 4:11-14)
⁵And if anyone wants to harm them, fire proceeds from their mouth and devours their enemies. And if anyone wants to harm them, he must be killed in this manner. (This shows that some will try to retake the temple mount, but will be instantly incinerated. See 2 Kings ch. 1) *⁶These have power to shut heaven, so that no rain falls in the days of their prophecy;*(Just as Elijah was able to do when God told him to, the same thing will happen during the tribulation. Remember, the world is already in a sad state before these two men start prophesying.) *And they have power over waters to turn them to blood, and to strike the earth with all plagues, as often as they desire.*

The world will have to pay attention to what the two witnesses say due to their miracles.

Here we have the keys to understanding how long the tribulation actually is. In **verse 2,** John is told that the Holy city will be trodden under foot by the Gentiles for **3.5 years.** Then in verse 3 John is told that the two witnesses will prophecy for **3.5 years.**

John also tells us that the antichrist will kill the two witnesses at the end of their ministry. So if the two witnesses' prophecy for **3.5 years,** and the beast will then rule over Jerusalem for **3.5 years,** that makes **7 years.**

In Daniel 9: 24-27 God tells us that **70 weeks** are determined for Israel. These weeks are not common weeks of **7 days each.** They are **7 years each.** If you study verse **25** you will see the time key. **69 weeks** are determined from the proclamation to **rebuild Jerusalem until Messiah,** Jesus, is **"cut off"** or killed. **69 times 7 equal 483.**

Jesus was killed exactly **483** years from the proclamation to rebuild Jerusalem.

So what about the **70ᵗʰ week?** In **verse 27** we are told that the antichrist will confirm a covenant with **Israel for one week**. The Bible says that he will confirm his covenant with many. Israel will be only one of many who will sign this treaty with the antichrist. The tribulation period is the seventieth week. From the point of the rapture on the Lords' attention is focused on Israel. The church is taken out of the way.

Elijah and Enoch prophesy to Israel. Although many will indeed be converted from other nations, their emphasis is on Israel alone. Consider the impact that these two men will have on the world.

Right after all hell has broken loose on this earth following the rapture and the earthquake, these two miracle workers will appear and preach Jesus to the people.

The fact that they appear to Israel will infuriate the Muslim community. Remember, Muhammad said Jesus had failed in His mission and Israel has had its last chance. The two witnesses will go against everything they hold dear. **Every basic doctrine of Islam is undone by the preaching of the cross of Jesus Christ.** There is no doubt that Enoch and Elijah, having been in heaven when Jesus left and when He returned will preach the truth about the Son of God!

*Rev 11:4 **These are the two olive trees and the two candlesticks, standing before the Lord of the earth.***

These two men are right now in Heaven. They are the two olive trees in **Zech. 4:1-14.** In Zechariah's day God said that these two men were in heaven. What two men are right now in Heaven that have never died? According to the Bible the only two that this could be talking about are **Enoch and Elijah.** Both of these men are still alive, Enoch prophesied about the end, and the book of Malachi says Elijah will come before the Day of the Lord. **Malachi 4:5** *behold, I will send you Elijah the prophet before the great and terrible day of Jehovah come.* John tells us that these two men prophesy in the city of Jerusalem. The entire city and nation will feel the effects of their ministry. The fact that they can stop rain from falling also means that the rain will fall where they want it to. I believe Israel will be blessed while the rest of the world suffers. Just as it happened in Egypt in the time of Moses, it will happen again.

THERE IS GOING TO BE A REVIVAL ON EARTH DURING THE TRIBULATION, CENTERED IN THE CITY OF JERUSALEM

The Greek word for witness is the word, "martoos" which means to give testimony like in a court of law. The two witnesses will give testimony to the earth about Jesus Christ being the <u>Son of God.</u> Interestingly enough, the Mosque on the Temple Mount has these words written on the front, <u>"He begetteth not nor was begotten"</u>, and this <u>"God, Who hath not taken unto Himself a son, and who hath no partner in the Sovereignty"</u>. In spite of the Islamic claims to the contrary, the two witnesses will mightily preach the true Gospel of Jesus Christ, the Son of the Living God.

Enoch and Elijah will come preaching to the Jews salvation thru **Jesus the true Messiah**. The devil knows this and is already working to negate their testimony. Yet their word will be with signs following. Fire will devour their adversaries and they will be able to turn the water into blood, withhold rain, and strike the earth as often as they want to.

Their word will not go unheeded by everyone, many will believe in their word concerning Jesus. By the large number of Christian Martyrs that are killed by the Muslims immediately after the two witness are killed it is obvious that millions of people around the world will believe in Jesus during this period of time.

This is after the rapture of the church! Yet even during this time God has a way of testifying to the world that Jesus is Lord! Thanks to modern communications, the whole world will watch and listen to the two witnesses' testimony.

For <u>3.5 years</u> no Muslim will be able to retake the city. **We are also told that the temple will be rebuilt at this time**. Enoch and Elijah will purify the temple mount area and the Jews will then rebuild the temple. Right now all of Islam would attack Israel if they even attempted to do such a thing. But when these two witnesses are <u>calling fire down</u> no one will be able to stop the rebuilding project.

Jesus said **<u>Elijah shall restore all things before the end</u>**. One of the things he restores is <u>the temple and temple worship.</u> **The new Sanhedrin recently met in Israel for the first time.** There are several organizations who are dedicated to seeing worship restored to the Temple Mount and a new Temple rebuilt. <u>The descendants of King David met in October of 2006 in New York.</u> Everything is ready for the restoration.

<u>Here is a direct quote from the Temple Mount Institute concerning the Ark of the Covenant;</u>

"This location is recorded in our sources, and today, there are those who know exactly<u> where this chamber is.</u> **And we know that the ark is still there**, undisturbed, and waiting for the day when it will be revealed. An attempt was made some few years ago to excavate towards the direction of this chamber, this resulted in widespread Moslem unrest and rioting.<u> They stand a great deal to lose if the Ark is revealed - for it will prove to the whole world that there really was a Holy Temple, and thus, that the Jews really do have a claim to the Temple Mount.</u> (The official position of the Islamic Wakf, the body that governs over the Temple Mount, is that there never was a Holy Temple, and that the Jews have no rights whatsoever to the place)".

Responding to a plan to build a synagogue on Judaism's most sacred site, Sheikh Raad Salah warns that the entire complex is Moslem. Islam was founded 550 years after the Jewish Temple was destroyed.

Sheikh Raad Salah - head of the **Islamic Movement** in Israel, a Hamas supporter, and an outspoken enemy of Israel - warns that Israeli plans to build a synagogue on the Temple Mount could lead to violence and bloodshed. <u>"The day will never come when a Moslem or an Arab will have the right to cede **even one foot** of the Al-Aqsa Mosque or of Jerusalem,"</u> the Sheikh's Al-Aqsa movement announced.

<u>Here is a quote from another Jewish group calling itself the Temple Mount Faithful Movement;</u>

"This exciting day will never be forgotten. It brought the Faithful Movement and all the people of Israel and their many friends from all over the world much closer to the godly desired moment of the rebuilding of the Temple and the coming of Mashiach ben David (Messiah, son of David). All of this is soon to happen, G-d willing, soon and in our lifetime.

Everyone in Israel and the world is called on to stand with, to encourage and to help the Temple Mount and Land of Israel Faithful Movement, spiritually and practically to fulfill her godly cause in our lifetime. Let us together open a great godly moral time in the life of

Israel and all the world. This cause is no longer a dream but it will soon be a practical reality in the life of all of us.

The Temple Mount Faithful Movement has started to prepare her Hanukkah march to the Temple Mount, the tombs of the Maccabees and Jerusalem together with the **cornerstones for the Third Temple.** This event was to take place on the **20th of December, 2006".** (The Israeli government stopped them.)

On the temple mount right now are two of Islam's holiest sights. The mosques that sit on the top of the mount make it impossible for the Jews to rebuild the temple without starting a war with every Muslim on earth. As proof, read this report from the Temple Mount Faithful Movement posted in November, 2006. "As Arutz-7 reported nearly two months ago, MK Uri Ariel (National Union) is preparing a plan for the construction of a synagogue on the southeastern corner of the Temple Mount. The plan must be approved by the Jerusalem municipality's planning committee - an unlikely eventuality - and Ariel is set to meet with rabbis and public figures on the issue later this week.

MK Ariel notes that such a building would "rectify a historic injustice," and that every Supreme Court ruling on the issue has recognized the right of every Jew to pray on the Temple Mount.

"The synagogue will not interfere with believing Moslems who wish to pray at the Al-Aqsa Mosque," Ariel said. "On the contrary, this is an opportunity for the Moslem world to demonstrate and prove that it is tolerant enough."

The "Moslem world" is not jumping at said opportunity. The announcement by Sheikh Salah's organization states, "We hereby warn aloud about the existence of a Jewish national consensus that is trying to build the Holy Temple at the expense of the Al-Aqsa Mosque. We warn that similar plans were submitted to Ariel Sharon and Ehud Barak and their publication led to violence, the ramifications of which have not ended to this day."

"The timing of the publication [of this plan] is not coincidental," the Islamic Movement states, "and it jibes with the increased calls for expulsion [of Arabs], the implementation of the policy of religious persecution and national discrimination, and the giving of a green light to the construction of the Third Temple."

"We remind, for the 1,000th time, that the entire Al-Aqsa mosque, including all of its area and alleys above the ground and under it, is exclusive and absolute Moslem property, and no one else has any rights to even one grain of earth in it."

"We remind the Israeli establishment, which stands behind these plans, that the problem of Al-Aqsa and Jerusalem is not just a Palestinian problem, but a <u>Palestinian, Arab and Islamic problem</u>. **The day the Al-Aqsa Mosque is harmed, Heaven forbid, all the Arab and Islamic nations will call to prevent this damage. Watch out! Beware of merely the thought of hurting or desecrating the mosque."**

As you can see, there is no room for compromise on the temple mount site.

Yet Elijah will restore all things and purify the temple mount area for 3.5 years. I believe that this will cause many Muslims to attack Israel. The battle will end on the hills of Israel as thousands of invaders are wiped out by the power of God thru Enoch and Elijah.

Islam can't stand idly by and let the Jews rebuild the temple. Yet there will not be much they can do as the two witnesses have such power to stop the rain from falling, turn their water to blood, and call down fire on anyone who disobeys their preaching.

What will the world will be like five minutes after the rapture? According to the Bible, many people will not only leave the earth due to the rapture, but many will die from the earthquake. Millions of people will be seeking answers, even the Muslims.

It will be hell on earth for those who miss the rapture. At the moment the antichrist steps on the scene, he will not be that distinguishable from any other leader except for his wisdom and way with words. He will speak great swelling words which will mesmerize his hearers. People looking for answers will definitely find them in him.

At the same time in Jerusalem, two men in cloaks will suddenly appear. These men will testify about Jesus to an unbelieving world where the entire true church is gone. Now there will be many millions of church going people left, but the true church will be gone. Probably no one would listen to these men except that they can do mighty miracles like calling fire down from heaven. I believe that these two witnesses will cleanse the Temple area. <u>The Jews will then re-institute ceremonial worship and rebuild the Temple.</u>

For 3.5 years the two witnesses will testify and will destroy any opposition to their message.

This tells us that not even the antichrist will go up against them for the first half of the tribulation period.

I believe that their testimonies will convert millions of people, including many Muslims. People want to believe that God is real and that He cares what happens to them. The two witnesses will definitely prove that.

Once again I want to say this; religion is the central focus of the book. God will find a way to reach everyone with the gospel of Jesus Christ during the tribulation period. For religious reasons many will never accept the truth even though God confirms the preaching with signs following. Yet in spite of it all many millions of desperate people will publicly accept Jesus as their personal Lord and Savior. For any who miss the rapture, this will be your only chance. The antichrist will be biding his time waiting for the opportune moment to strike the two witnesses and retake Jerusalem.

The first 3.5 years of the tribulation will be marked by aggressive testimonials of the power of God to save mankind thru Jesus.

The second half of the Tribulation will be known as the **great Tribulation.** The antichrist will be fully unleashed and will institute new worship forcefully on the earth. The mark will ensure only good Muslims will be able to buy or sell. Only the Jews and a scattering of Christians will resist.

Chapter eight

Understanding Who The Antichrist Is

Rev. 13:1-2

Then he stood on the sand of the sea. And I saw a beast rising up out of the sea, **having seven heads** and **ten horns,** and on his horns ten crowns, and on his heads a blasphemous name. <u>²Now the beast which I saw was like a leopard, his feet were like the feet of a bear, and his mouth like the mouth of a lion.</u> The dragon gave him **his power, his throne,** and **great authority**.

Just who is the antichrist? He has some very definite characteristics.

1. Part leopard
2. Part bear
3. Part lion

In the book of **Daniel, chapter 7,** Daniel saw three great beast rise out of the sea. The first was like a lion. The second was like a bear. The third was like a leopard.

The interpretation was this:

1. The <u>Lion</u> was Babylon
2. The <u>Bear</u> was Medo-Persia
3. The <u>Leopard</u> was Greece, which included modern Turkey

According to **Isaiah chapter 14:24-27;** God says He will break the Assyrian in the land of Israel. Where was Assyria? It is in present day northern Iraq and Syria. What common things linked the three kingdoms Daniel saw? They all conquered Jerusalem.

I believe that scripture shows us that the antichrist will come from the area of Iraq or Syria. He will come in speaking great things. He will have answers to the many problems that mankind will be facing.

Ninevah was the capital of the Assyrian empire. It is now in northern Iraq. However the capital was at various times located in different cities such as Babylon.

The Assyrian empire was perhaps the **most blood-thirsty empire** that ever existed. Religion played a large part in their society. **Forced conversion was normal**. Every conquered nation had to bow down to the Assyrian gods. The Assyrians believed it was divine destiny that they conquered all nations and forced them to accept the gods of Assyria. Anyone who refused was destroyed where they stood.

In Assyria women were treated little better than cattle and could be divorced for any reason. They were forced to wear a veil at all times and those who were not veiled were considered to be prostitutes. They could be killed if they were even accused or suspected of committing adultery.

These very same archaic morals are common today throughout Islam. So-called revenge killings are still common among Muslims today. A father will kill his own daughter if she is even suspected of committing adultery. Often the whole village will turn out to witness it.

Understanding who the Bible says Jesus will destroy when He returns at Armageddon.

The great image and the two feet and the ten toes.

Dan 2:31-45 Thou, O king, sawest, and, behold, a great image. This image, which was mighty, and whose brightness was excellent, stood before thee; and the aspect thereof was terrible.

As for this image,**#1 its head** was of fine gold,**#2 its breast and its arms** of silver, its **#3belly and its thighs** of brass,

#4its legs of iron, #5 its feet part of iron, and part of clay. Thou saw till **that a stone** was cut out without hands, **which smote the image upon its feet that were of iron and clay,** and brake them in pieces. Then was the iron, the clay, the brass, the silver, and the gold, **broken in pieces together,** and became like the chaff of the summer threshing-floors; and the wind carried them away, so that no place was found for them: and the stone that smote the image **became a great mountain,** and **filled the whole earth.**

This is the dream; and we will tell the interpretation thereof before the king.

Thou, O king, art king of kings, unto whom the God of heaven hath given the kingdom, the power, and the strength, and the glory. And wherever the children of men dwell, the beasts of the field and the birds of the heavens hath he given into thy hand, and hath made thee to rule over them all: **thou art the head of gold.**

And after thee shall arise another kingdom inferior to thee; and another third kingdom of brass, which shall bear rule over all the earth. And the fourth kingdom shall be strong as iron, forasmuch as iron breaketh in pieces and subdueth all things; and as iron that crusheth all these, shall it break in pieces and crush.

And whereas thou sawest the feet and toes, part of potters' clay, and part of iron, **it shall be a divided kingdom**; but there shall be in it of the strength of the iron, forasmuch as thou sawest the iron mixed with miry clay. And as the toes of the feet were part of iron, and part of clay, so the kingdom shall be partly strong, and partly broken.

And whereas thou sawest the iron mixed with miry clay, they shall **mingle themselves (Hebrew-ARAB)** with the seed of men; but they shall not cleave one to another, even as iron doth not mingle with clay. And in the days of those kings shall the God of heaven set up a kingdom which shall never be destroyed, nor shall the sovereignty thereof be left to another people; but it shall break in pieces and consume **all these kingdoms**, and it shall stand for ever. Forasmuch as thou sawest that a stone was cut out of the mountain without hands, and that it brake in pieces the iron, the brass, the clay, the silver, and the gold; the great God hath made known to the king what shall come to pass hereafter: and the dream is certain, and the interpretation thereof sure.

The first four kingdoms conquered Jerusalem and Judea, the Arab empire of the antichrist will also.
1. Babylon
2. Medes and Persians
3. Greeks, which included Asia Minor- Turkey
4. Rome
5. Arab empire
6. The Kingdom of Jesus Christ

There are two feet; showing that there are two main divisions in Islam, Sunni and Shiite.

The stone hit the image at the last days. Literally at the end of days all five empires will be in existence in opposition to the Lord because He destroys them.

THE TEN TOES- **REVELATION 17:12 And the ten horns that thou sawest are ten kings, who have received no kingdom as yet; but they receive authority as kings, with the beast, for one hour.**

Verse 34; The stone struck the image at its feet and toes, the Arab empire and brought all empires down.

Jeremiah 25:15-26 the nations God will destroy.

Jer 25:15 For thus saith Jehovah, the God of Israel, unto me: take this cup of the wine of wrath at my hand, and cause all the nations, to whom I send thee, to drink it.

Jer 25:16 And they shall drink, and reel to and fro, and be mad, because of the sword that I will send among them.

Jer 25:17 Then took I the cup at Jehovah's hand, and made all the nations to drink, unto whom Jehovah had sent me:

Jer 25:18 to wit, Jerusalem, and the cities of Judah, and the kings thereof, and the princes thereof, to make them a desolation, an astonishment, a hissing, and a curse, as it is this day;

Jer 25:19 Pharaoh king of Egypt, and his servants, and his princes, and all his people;

Jer 25:20 and all the mingled people (- in Hebrew it says "The Arabs"), and all the kings of the land of the Uz (eastern Arabia- the regions of Kuwait to Qatar and the UAE), and all the kings of the Philistines, and Ashkelon, and Gaza, and Ekron, and the remnant of Ashdod; (-Palestinians)

Jer 25:21 Edom (south of Judah, Sinai and part of Saudi Arabia), and Moab (Jordan) , and the children of Ammon (Syria);

Jer 25:22 and all the kings of Tyre, and all the kings of Sidon(Lebanon), and the kings of the isle which is beyond the sea(North coast of Africa-Lybia)

Jer 25:23 Dedan (Sudan), and Tema (child of Ishmael), and Buz, (Abrahams' brothers son, he lived in modern day Iraq). And all that have the corners of their hair cut off;

Jer 25:24 and all the kings of Arabia, and all the kings of the mingled people (Hebrew says Arabs) that dwell in the wilderness; (Saudi Arabia) Jer 25:25 and all the kings of Zimri (Child of Abraham,) and all the kings of Elam, and all the kings of the Medes; (Persia-Iran) Jer 25:26 and all the kings of the north, far and near, one with another; and all the kingdoms of the world, which are upon the face of the earth: and the king of Sheshach (Babylon) shall drink after them.

Notice something about these nations; **they are all Muslim.**

They act insane, they are Mad. They are insane with hate. Sheshach is another name for Babylon. **The prince that is to come.**

Dan 9:26b and the people of the prince that shall come shall destroy the city and the sanctuary;

Many say that because the Roman army under General Titus destroyed the sanctuary, then it is a Roman or European who is the antichrist. Actually, he led the army, but the people were not Roman. Josephus explains who was with the Roman army in "Wars of the Jews" 3:4

"But as to Titus, he sailed over from Achaia to Alexandria, there finding his father, together with the two legions, the fifth and the tenth, which were the most eminent legions of all, he joined them to that fifteenth legion which was with his father; eighteen cohorts followed these legions; there came also five cohorts from Cesarea, with one troop of horsemen, and five other troops of horsemen from Syria. Now these ten cohorts had severally a thousand footmen, but the other thirteen cohorts had no more than six hundred footmen apiece, with a hundred and twenty horsemen. There were also a considerable number of auxiliaries got together, that came from the kings Antiochus, and Agrippa, and Sohemus, each of them contributing one thousand footmen that were archers, and a thousand horsemen. Malchus also, the king of Arabia, sent a thousand horsemen, besides five thousand footmen, the greatest part of which were archers; so that the whole army, including the auxiliaries sent by the kings, as well horsemen as footmen, when all were united together, amounted to sixty thousand, besides the servants, who, as they followed in vast numbers, so because they had been trained up in war with the rest, ought not to be distinguished from the fighting men".

These men were from **areas that are today completely Muslim.** They are the people of the prince that should come.

The Roman army was not just manned by Romans; in fact much of any Roman legion was filled with people from other nations.

Because of the location, the neighbors of Judah sent troops to assist in the defeat and destruction of Jerusalem and the temple.

The people of the prince that is to come-the people from the Muslim nations- did have a hand in destroying the city and temple. So we see that it was mainly people from what are today Muslim nations that attacked and destroyed Jerusalem. These nations and tribes will unite under a man that the Bible calls Sheshach the king of Babylon.

Here is the definition of the beast, notice the similarity between him and the devil.

Rev. 13:1 Then he stood on the sand of the sea. And I saw a beast rising up out of the sea, **having seven heads** and **ten horns,** and on **his horns ten crowns**, and on **his heads a blasphemous name**.

Rev. 12:3 And another sign appeared in heaven: behold, a great, fiery **red dragon** (the devil) having **seven heads** and **ten horns,** and seven diadems on his heads.

There has always been the teaching that the Bible says the beast sits on seven mountains and therefore the place he rules from must be Rome. Rome was known as the city on seven hills. It makes sense until you actually read what the Bible says.

Rev. 17:9-12 Here is the mind which has wisdom: **The seven heads are seven mountains on which the woman sits.** [10]These are also seven kings. Five have fallen, one is, and the other has not yet come. And when he comes, he must continue a short time. [11]And the beast that was, and is not, is himself also the eighth, and is of the seven, and is going to perdition. [12]**The ten horns which you saw are ten kings** who have received no kingdom as yet, but they receive authority for one hour as kings with the beast.

It is the woman that rides the beast to power that is described as sitting on seven mountains which are seven kings. These kings or rulers are eventually supplanted by the antichrists' devoted followers at the end of the tribulation.

This would make it appear that he makes war on the Sunni nations and appoints his own people to rule over them. If so it only proves the violence of the antichrist.

Here is the Contemporary English Versions reading; **Rev 17:9** Anyone with wisdom can figure this out. The seven heads that the woman is sitting on stand for seven hills. **These heads are also seven kings.**

Unless Rome was ruled by seven kings it certainly does not qualify.

Rev. 17:10. Five have fallen, one is, and the other has not yet come. And when he comes, he must continue a short time.

In Johns day there had been 12 Caesars of Rome. So that rules out the Romans. What was the system of government that the woman ruled over? According to Islam, there were four Caliphs after Muhammad. These four plus Muhammad equals **five.**

Rev. 17:10-11 Five have fallen, one is, and the other has not yet come. And when he comes, he must continue a short time. [11]And the beast that was, and is not, **is himself also the eighth, and is of the seven**, and is going to perdition.

Does Islam have a teaching about eight leaders? Yes the Ismaili group calling itself the Seveners teaches that the last Imam would be the eighth and final Imam. They are a branch of the Shiites.

They differ from regular Shiites only in the counting of the Imams. The Shiites teach that there were twelve Imams, with the twelfth being hidden by God until the last days. The Ismailis teach that he is the eighth.

The Isma'ilis are called Seveners because they believe Isma'il, Ja'far's eldest son, to be his father's true successor and the seventh and last Imam who is now in occultation (in hiding,) but who will one day return to earth as the Mahdi to usher in a golden age.

The Isma'ilis integrated into their belief system ideas taken from Jewish and Christian mysticism, Gnosticism, Manichaeism, Neo-Platonism, Hinduism and Buddhism.

Ismailis hold to most Shia doctrines such as the nature of truth and the divine inspiration of Imams. According to Shiite and Ismaili teaching, anyone can tell any lie and it is not a sin if it protects them or Islam. Both branches believe the Imam is of a divine origin.

WHERE GOG AND MAGOG CAME FROM:

Gen 10:1 Now these are the generations of the sons of Noah, Shem, Ham, and Japheth: and unto them were sons born after the flood.

Gen 10:2 The sons of Japheth; **Gomer,** and **Magog,** and Madai, and Javan, and **Tubal**, and **Meshech**, and Tiras.

Gen 10:3 And the sons of Gomer; Ashkenaz, and Riphath, and **Togarmah. (These are all known places, and today they are Muslim.)**

Gen 10:4 And the sons of Javan; Elishah, and Tarshish, Kittim, and Dodanim.

Gen 10:5 **By these were the isles of the Gentiles divided in their lands**; every one after his tongue, after their families, in their nations. **(These are the northern nations, those to the north of Iraq and Iran, the old soviet nations which are all Muslim)**

Gen 10:6 And the sons of Ham; Cush(**Ethiopia)**, and Mizraim, and Phut, and Canaan. **The nation that is still called the Land of Ham to this day is Egypt.** (Muslim)

Gen 10:7 And the sons of Cush; Seba, and Havilah, and Sabtah, and Raamah, and Sabtecha: and the sons of Raamah; Sheba, **(ARABIA)** (Muslim) and Dedan **(SUDAN).** (Muslim)

Gen 10:8 And Cush begat Nimrod: he began to be a mighty one in the earth.

Gen 10:9 He was a mighty hunter before the LORD: wherefore it is said, Even as Nimrod the mighty hunter before the LORD.

Gen 10:10 **And the beginning of his kingdom was Babel, (Iraq.)**

Ezekiel

Eze 38:2 Son of man, set thy face against Gog, the land of Magog, the chief prince of Meshech and Tubal, and prophesy against him,

Eze 38:3 And say, Thus saith the Lord GOD; Behold, I am against thee, O Gog, the chief prince of Meshech and Tubal **(these are areas of modern day Turkey)** (Muslim)

Eze 38:4 And I will turn thee back, and put hooks into thy jaws, and I will bring thee forth, and all thine army, horses and horsemen, all of them clothed with all sorts of armour, even a great company with bucklers and shields, all of them handling swords:

Eze 38:5 **Persia, (Iran)** (Muslim) **Ethiopia**,(Muslim) and **Libya**(Muslim) with them; all of them with shield and helmet:

Eze 38:6 Gomer, (Muslim) and all his bands; **the house of Togarmah of the north quarters**, (Muslim) and all his bands: and many people with thee.

Eze 38:13 Sheba **(Arabia)**, (Muslim) and Dedan **(Sudan)**, (Muslim) and the merchants of Tarshish **(Along the Southern Mediterranean Coast)**, (Muslim) with all the young lions thereof, shall say unto thee, Art thou come to take a spoil? hast thou gathered thy company to take a prey? To carry away silver and gold, to take away cattle and goods, to take a great spoil?

Daniel 11:43 But he shall have power over the treasures of gold and of silver, and over all the precious things of Egypt: (Muslim) and the Libyans(Muslim) and the Ethiopians(Muslim) shall be at his steps.

Eze 38:2 Son of man, set thy face against Gog, the land of Magog, the chief prince of Meshech. (Chief Prince here is the word "Rosh". Many have tried to prove that this is Russia. However the word Rosh is Hebrew and simply means "The Head", or the leader. The word is still used today for the Jewish New Year, "Rosh Hoshana".

Kingdoms and Mountains

In the Bible many times when the word mountain is used it denotes a kingdom. **Dan 2:35** Then was the iron, the clay, the brass, the silver, and the gold, broken to pieces together, and became like the chaff of the summer threshing floors; and the wind carried them away, that no place was found for them: and the stone that smote the image **became a great mountain**, and filled the whole earth. See also Isaiah 2:2-3, 11:9, 25:10, 27:13, 57:11, 65:25, and 66:20.

Five have fallen and one is could also mean this; five kingdoms have fallen, one is now alive and one is coming. What kingdoms would this be talking about? 1. Egypt, 2.Assyria, 3.Babylon, 4.Persia, 5.Greece, 6.Rome, 7.the Islamic Ottoman Empire makes for seven empires or mountains. The Ottomans ruled until the twentieth century. A revived empire could very well be what is coming. This new Islamic empire will not be based in Turkey. Its base will be in the ancient region of Babylon.

Rev 13:2 <u>And the beast which I saw was like unto a leopard, and his feet were as the feet of a bear, and his mouth as the mouth of a lion.</u> It will quickly take over other territories like Greece did under Alexander. It will have many millions of soldiers as did the Persians. It will have a mouth speaking great things like king Nebuchadnezzar of Babylon. **Dan 4:30** <u>The king spoke, and said, Is not this great Babylon, that I have built for the house of the kingdom by the might of my power, and for the honor of my majesty?</u>

Nebuchadnezzar's boast is similar to the antichrist' boast in **Isaiah 14:13-14** "For thou hast said in thine heart, I will ascend into heaven, I will exalt my throne above the stars of God: I will sit also upon the mount of the congregation, in the sides of the north: I will ascend above the heights of the clouds; I will be like the most High". His mouth will get him into trouble.

Isaiah 46:1 Bel boweth down, **(Bel was the title of the chief Babylonian god, not his name)** Nebo stoopeth, **(Nebo means literally "the Prophet". What name is always associated with Muhammad? He is known "the prophet". He is called the last prophet of god.)** Their idols were upon the beasts, and upon the cattle: **Judges 8:21** Then Zebah and Zalmunna said, Rise thou, and fall upon us: for as the man is, so is his strength. And Gideon arose, and slew Zebah and Zalmunna, and took away the ornaments **(Hebrew is "sahharone" which means a crescent moon ornament)** that were on their camels' necks.

The Middle East is at war at the beginning of the tribulation according to Islamic prophecies.

At the beginning of the tribulation, while most nations are attempting to dig out of the ruins, the Muslims will see the destruction of the world system as proof of Allah's power. What has up until now been a cry for Shari a law will then become a shout. Remember, the Muslims expect a massive destruction of some sort to come to this world before the end time.

<u>Of all major religions on earth, only Islam has so little respect for life.</u> To die or kill means very little. Christians and Jews believe that we are made in the image of God, therefore we should value each person. Muslims feel that man is of no value unless he totally agrees

with the Muslim religious idea. Just what a true Muslim is can change dramatically from person to person.

To understand Islam you have to understand tribal life in Arabia 1,400 years ago, because that is what Islam is based on. <u>Basically, Muslim nations of the Middle East are nothing more than tribes or clans.</u> They are not nations in the sense we think. They still hold to ancient creeds and values handed down from father to son. Nothing has changed in Islam except what the outside world has brought in. Islam doesn't breed change, only stagnation.

The wars that are taking place in the Middle East are only a prelude to what is coming. **Jesus said that there would be wars and rumors of wars but the end is not immediate**.

As soon as the economy of the world is shut down after the rapture by a massive quake, the power hungry tyrants of the world will launch attacks against their neighbors in an attempt to make an empire for themselves.

Also Jesus said that "**nation would rise against nation**", which in Greek says "**ethnic against ethnic**". Racial wars will erupt across the world. Not just black on white, but tribe on tribe, class against class, **hatred that is just below the surface** will spill out on that day.

The Muslims have many grudges to settle among themselves. Old divisions are still there and will be the catalyst for killing. Neither America nor any other nation will be able to bring peace to the Middle East. Islam doesn't cause peace, only war and strife. It simply is designed to cause division and death.

The ten Kings that rule for one hour.

These men serve the Mahdi. They will vow allegiance to him and do whatsoever he tells them to do. As puppet kings they will have one mind and will follow the rulings of their puppet master. Just as the Mahdi will follow the leading of satan, and the false Jesus will follow the Mahdi, these men will fall in line behind him to do his will.

Here is a quote from a Hadith concerning the last days according to Muslims prophecy;

"After the death of a Ruler there will be some dispute between the people. At that time a citizen of Medina will flee and go to Mecca. While in Mecca, certain people will approach him between Hajrul Sawad and Maqaame Ibraheem, and forcefully pledge their allegiance to him.

Thereafter a huge army will proceed from Syria to attack him but when they will be at Baida, which is between Mecca and Medina; they will be swallowed into the ground.

On seeing this, the Abdaals of Shaam (Damascus) as well as large numbers of people from Iraq will come to him and pledge their allegiance to him. Then a person from Quraish, (Saudi Arabia) whose uncle will be from the Bani Kalb tribe, will send an army to attack him, only to be overpowered, by the will of Allah.

This defeated army will be that of the Bani Kalb. Unfortunate indeed is he who does not receive a share from the booty of the Kalb. This person will distribute the spoils of war after the battle. He will lead the people according to the Sunnat and during his reign Islam will spread throughout the world".

Now I will compare this passage to Daniel chapter 11. I will mark the Muslim prophecies with a capital letter **"M"**.

"M" After the death of a Ruler there will be some dispute between the people. (This speaks of a recognized leader in Islam who will die. **Daniel 11:18 And he shall turn his face to the coastlands, and shall capture many. But a ruler shall make cease his reproach for him, but his reproach will return to him. 11:19 And he shall turn his face to the fortresses of his land. But he shall stumble and fall, and shall not be found.** After he dies the people will have a war to determine the next leader.

11:20 And one who sends an exacter shall stand in his place, for the glory of the kingdom. But within few days he shall be broken, not in anger nor in battle.

Someone will try to take the kingdom but will not live long enough to do anything except tax the people.) **M.** At that time a citizen of

Medina will flee and go to Mecca. While in Mecca, certain people will approach him between Hajrul Sawad and Maqaame Ibraheem, and forcefully pledge their allegiance to him.(**Daniel 11:21 And a despised one shall stand up in his place, and they shall not give to him the honor of the king; but he will enter while at ease and seize the kingdom by intrigues.**

11:22 And the forces of the overflow will be swept from before him, and they will be broken, and also the ruler of a covenant.)

"M". Thereafter a huge army will proceed from Syria to attack him but when they will be at Baida, which is between Mecca and Medina; they will be swallowed into the ground.

(The Muslims will be divided on the Mahdi. The Shiites will accept him much quicker than the Sunnis will.) **"M"** On seeing this, the Abdaals of Shaam as well as large numbers of people from Iraq will come to him and pledge their allegiance to him. (This is the Shiite area. Clearly the Shiites are looking for the Mahdi and will take his victory against overwhelming odds as proof that he is their long awaited deliverer.)

"M" Then a person from Quraish, whose uncle will be from the Bani Kalb tribe, will send an army to attack him, only to be overpowered, by the will of Allah. This defeated army will be that of the Bani Kalb. Unfortunate indeed is he who does not receive a share from the booty of the Kalb. (The Bani Kalb are from the area of what is today Saudi Arabia. These are the Sunni Muslims who now control Mecca and Medina.)

"M" This person will distribute the spoils of war after the battle. (Daniel **11:24 He shall enter peaceably even upon the fattest places of the province; and he shall do that which his fathers have not done, nor his fathers' fathers; he shall scatter among them the prey, and spoil, and riches.) "M"** He will lead the people according to the Sunnat and during his reign Islam will spread throughout the world. He will remain seven years.

(Daniel 9:27 says that the antichrist will confirm the covenant for seven years, not make it, but he will break it after 3.5 years.)

This talks about the coming war between Islam. Many of the Muslims will fight and kill each other as they try to seize power at the beginning of the tribulation. Shiite and Sunni Muslims will war on each other as the tribes and nations seek to take control.

Even now the Muslims are at war with each other. Whether Sunni, Shiite or other, they have always been at war between themselves. When the end time comes and the U.S is no longer the enemy to fight with, these nations and tribes will turn on each other as they jockey for position in the new world order. The purity of Islam is the goal of the Mahdi. He will decide what is truly pure.

Dan 9:27 And he shall confirm the covenant with many for one week: and in the midst of the week he shall cause the sacrifice and the oblation to cease, and for the overspreading of **abominations he shall make it desolate**, even until the consummation, and that determined shall be poured upon the desolate. The "Awful Horror" or "abomination that makes desolate" is the image of the beast. It will stay in the temple area where the altar was. Instead of sacrificing to God, people will enter the temple to worship at the feet of the statue of the Mahdi.

Dan 11:22-24 and the forces of the overflow will be swept from before him, and they will be broken, and also the ruler of a covenant. (The ruler of the covenant would be the two witnesses. The antichrist will make a peace treaty or "covenant" with Israel for seven years. When he breaks the covenant he will literally sweep away all resistance.)

And after they join him, he will practice deceit. For he will come and be strong with a few people. (His strength will come from the devil himself. Therefore he will be able to deceive his enemies. It is clear that many of the Muslim rulers will resist him. Their resistance will only serve to infuriate the Mahdi. He will practice deceit. His goal is to exact revenge on his adversaries.

He shall enter safely, even into the rich places of the province. (This speaks of Israel). And he shall do what his fathers have not done, nor his fathers' fathers. He shall plunder, and spoil, and scatter goods among them.

(Let me quote from Muhammad here; **"this person (Imam Mahdi) will distribute the spoils of war after the battle."** The Mahdi will give all of his followers much reward for their service. Unlike the present regimes of the Middle East, he will share his wealth.) And he shall devise his plots against the strongholds, even for a time.

Daniel 11:36-39 and the king shall do according **to his will**. (Much like satan before him he will not be willing to allow anyone else to receive glory. The devil was not willing to give glory to God but wanted it for himself. The antichrist Mahdi will be deceived by the devil and the false Jesus. The false Jesus will glorify the Mahdi until he makes the Mahdi to believe that he really is god in the flesh.) *And he* ___*shall exalt and magnify himself above every god*___, (in his delusion he will see no one who can resist him. This will make him feel unbeatable. After all, he defeated death when he was struck by a sword and yet lived. This will only fuel his self-obsession.) *And shall speak marvelous things against the God of gods, and shall prosper until the fury is fulfilled. For that which is decreed shall be done.*

He will not regard the ___**God of his fathers**___, (this speaks of the Islam of his fathers. The Mahdi will not recognize it as pure. He will institute a new religious world order. Only thru the Mahdi will life and prosperity be possible.

Nor the desire of women, (this has led many to assume that the antichrist is a homosexual. It does not necessarily mean that. The Hebrew word literally means "tenderness of women" which describes a harsh treatment of women. *Nor regard any god. For he shall magnify himself above all.* (Just as the devil was self-absorbed to the point where he no longer magnified God, the Mahdi will also feel that he has earned his place in paradise.)

But in his place he shall honor the god of forces ;(literally means that he will be so secure in his seeming invincibility that he will not feel the need of a god.)

And a god whom his fathers did not know, he shall honor with gold and silver, and with precious stones and desirable things. (This god is the statue of the Mahdi which will reside inside the third temple in Jerusalem. It will be literally a god whom his fathers did not know.)

So he shall act in the fortresses of the strongholds with a strange god, whom he shall acknowledge. He shall multiply in glory, and he shall cause them to rule over many, and shall divide the land for a price. This speaks of the ten kings which will rule with him for one hour. They will sell their souls to the Mahdi. He will appoint them to rule over the nations that he has conquered. His reason for doing this is to destroy Sunni Islam and forcibly replace it with his own version, one dedicated to him.

If all the Middle East is Muslim, why do they constantly war on each other? Because hate is their life and you can't simply stop when your god commands you to hate.

In the midst of their fighting one will emerge different from the rest. This will be their Mahdi, the antichrist. He will overcome by peace. According to their prophecies, he will leave Mecca for Medina where he will be approached by Muslims who will force him to be their leader.

Then after he accepts, a large army from Syria will attack him. They will be destroyed as will another army of Arabs. At this time many from Iraq, Iran (Shiites) and other places will swear allegiance to him.

I believe that he will in fact be a Shiite Muslim or even perhaps from the sect of Shiites known as Ismailis.

The reason I feel he may be an Ismailite is that they teach that the Mahdi will be divine. The antichrist sets himself in the temple of God, showing himself that he is God.

Many false prophets will claim to be the one. One of these politicians who will arise will be the antichrist. Probably the Arabs would have already conquered Jerusalem except that God sends **two messengers.**

Why the antichrist makes a peace treaty with Israel. Here is a quote attributed to Muhammad, <u>"There will be four peace agreements between you and the Romans (Christians). The fourth agreement will be mediated through a person who will be from the progeny of Hadhrat Haroon</u> **and will be upheld for seven years."** The Muslims will see this as a fulfillment of their prophecies, not ours.

No Muslim wants to make a peace treaty with Israel, yet they can, according to Islam, if it furthers Islam or if it gains them an advantage later on. The only reason the antichrist agrees to the treaty is because the two witnesses give Israel negotiating power. The antichrist will be weak starting out and unable to resist them. He will settle on a diplomatic solution for the time being until he can kill them.

Due to their weakness the Arabs will sign a treaty, but it will be with the Nation of Israel. The two witnesses are dealing with the religious issues of the day; they do not deal with political problems as such. This treaty will be broken in the midst of the tribulation by the antichrist and the false prophet.

THE MARCH ON THE TEMPLE MOUNT TO KILL THE TWO WITNESSES

For the first 3.5 years of the tribulation period, the antichrist will be able to institute his economic program on the world due to his enormous oil wealth. After 3.5 years of not being able to retake the temple mount, he will raise an army and prepare to march on Jerusalem.

It is at this time that the **false Jesus** appears to the Muslim armies. They are expecting him to kill the prophets in Jerusalem, who they call the Dajjil. Again according to Islamic teaching, Jesus will come back to earth where he will prove that he was never crucified.

After submitting himself to the Mahdi, he will personally kill the two prophets as well as many thousands of Jews who follow them.

Here is where the 144 thousand witnesses will come into the scene. As followers of the two witnesses I believe the 144,000 will teach the truth about Jesus in neighboring countries. This will result in their beheadings. Dying as martyrs for Christ they will ascend to His very presence. **Jesus witnessed on earth for 3.5 years and so will the two witnesses.**

According to Islam, their Jesus will outlaw all other religions except Islam as he interprets it. Anyone who will not convert will die by beheading. He will cause all people to worship the antichrist, even other Muslims. This false Jesus will follow the Mahdi-antichrist, submitting himself to the antichrist in every way. He will do many miracles in the presence of the antichrist to prove that he is Jesus. The false Jesus will not have marks of crucifixion on his body like the real Jesus does. He will seek to verify the Muslim claim that Jesus was never crucified.

RELIGION IS THE DRIVING FORCE BEHIND THE ENDTIMES.

The antichrist will come into power due to his religion. There are right now millions of Muslims who will gladly pledge allegiance to him if he can give them victory over the church and Jews. God planned all of this long before Muhammad was born. It is the plan of God for two major religions to square off in the final conflict.

Today in the Muslim community there is a saying, "first comes Saturday and then comes Sunday". What they mean by this is first they kill the Jews, and then they kill the Christians. Killing and hating are as natural to them as breathing.

Here is a quote from the Koran concerning the Muslim view of the end times. In Chapter "Fitnah" of Mishkah al Masabih, **Mohammed says: "The last hour will not come before the Muslims fight the Jews and the Muslims kill them, so that Jews will hide behind stones and trees and the stone and the tree will say, "O Muslim, O servant of God! There is a Jew behind me; come and kill him."."**

Most expositors of the Bible focus on the political issues that bring the antichrist to power. I think we miss the obvious truth. **It is not politics that allows the antichrist to gain a following, it is religion.** Every thing he will do is magnified by the religious expectation concerning him.

Israel is vulnerable today. If God doesn't intervene they will cease to exist. Yet **God does intervene**, again and again He delivers them. At the moment of the rapture the two witnesses will appear in Jerusalem. God again brings deliverance to the Jews.

Revelation 11:7-13 (ASV)

*7 (ASV) and when they shall have **finished their testimony**, the beast that cometh up out of the abyss shall make war with them, and overcome them, and kill them.* **(Antichrist assisted by the false prophet Jesus)**
8 And their dead bodies lie in the street of the great city, which spiritually is called Sodom and Egypt, where also their Lord was crucified. **(Jerusalem)**
9 And from among the peoples and tribes and tongues and nations do men look upon their dead bodies three days and a half, and suffer not their dead bodies to be laid in a tomb. (The Muslims in Mogadishu paraded our dead soldiers in the streets and rejoiced over them, much the same way that these people will do to the two witnesses)
10 And they that dwell on the earth rejoice over them, and make merry; and they shall send gifts one to another; because these two prophets tormented them that dwell on the earth.
11 And after the three days and a half the breath of life from God entered into them, and they stood upon their feet; and great fear fell upon them that

beheld them. (For all their hate, they are still just people and the fear of God is in them somewhere).

¹² And they heard a great voice from heaven saying unto them, Come up hither. And they went up into heaven in the cloud; and their enemies beheld them. (TV cameras will record this. The antichrist will have to make this out to be a trick of the devil so he can keep their faith in him).

¹³ And in that hour there was a great earthquake, and the tenth part of the city fell; and there were killed in the earthquake seven thousand persons: and the rest were affrighted, and gave glory to the God of heaven. (Fear of God is in their hearts no matter what comes out of their mouths)

The two witnesses will resurrect from the dead after three and a half days and go up to heaven in the sight of the entire world. At the time that the Muslims are celebrating their victory, God sends a great earthquake upon the city. Ten percent of the city will be destroyed. The Muslim section will receive the punishment of God although they will not acknowledge Him.

Think about the entire world watching on TV as Enoch and Elijah resurrect. For those who will be celebrating and giving gifts to each other this will cause them to greatly fear. One moment they felt happy and the very next moment these two prophets arose!

Chapter nine

The woman and who she is

Rev. 12:1-5

*Now a great sign appeared in heaven: a woman clothed with the sun, with the moon under her feet, and on her head a garland of twelve stars.(****Genesis 37:9****) ²Then being with child, she cried out in labor and in pain to give birth. ³And another sign appeared in heaven: behold, a great, fiery red dragon having* **seven heads and ten horns,** *and seven diadems on his heads. ⁴****His tail drew a third of the stars of heaven and threw them to the earth.*** *And the dragon stood before the woman who was ready to give birth, to devour her Child as soon as it was born. ⁵She bore a male Child who was to rule all nations with a rod of iron. And her Child was caught up to God and His throne.*

Rev. 12:6

Then the woman fled into the wilderness, where she has a place prepared by God that they should feed her there one thousand two hundred and sixty days (3.5years).

Rev. 12:13-17

Now when the dragon saw that he had been cast to the earth, he persecuted the woman who gave birth to the male Child. ¹⁴But the woman was given two wings of a great eagle, that she might fly into the wilderness to her place, where she is nourished for a time and times and half a time **(3.5 years)** *from the presence of the serpent. ¹⁵So the serpent spewed water out of his mouth like a flood after the woman that he might cause her to be carried away by the flood.*

¹⁶But the earth helped the woman and the earth opened its mouth and swallowed up the flood which the dragon had spewed out of his mouth **(this means that his first attempts at conquering Israel will fail).**

¹⁷And the **dragon was enraged with the woman,** *and he went to make war with the rest of her offspring, who keep the commandments of God* *and have the testimony of Jesus Christ,*(he hates the true Jews. according to Paul in **Romans 2:28-29** *For he is not a Jew who is one outwardly, nor is circumcision that outwardly in flesh; **but he is a Jew who is one inwardly,** and circumcision is of the heart; in spirit and not in letter; whose praise is not from men, but from God.* A true Jew is a Christian)

The first thing to understand of course is who the child is. <u>Some insist that the child must be the church or Israel.</u> There is really no doubt who it is referring to if you compare scriptures. There is only one who will rule the nations with a rod of iron. ***Jesus is the child.***

Psalms 2:6-9
6 *(NKJV)* *"Yet I have set My King on My holy hill of Zion."*
7 *"I will declare the decree: The Lord has said to Me, '**You are My Son, Today I have begotten You.***
8 *Ask of Me, and I will give You the nations for Your inheritance, And the ends of the earth for Your possession.*
9 ***You shall break them with a rod of iron;*** *You shall dash them to pieces like a potter's vessel.'*

<u>*"Isaiah 11:1-4*</u>
1 *there shall come forth a **Rod** from the stem of Jesse, and a Branch shall grow out of his roots.*
2 *The Spirit of the Lord shall rest upon Him, the Spirit of wisdom and understanding, The Spirit of counsel and might, The Spirit of knowledge and of the fear of the Lord.*
3 *His delight is in the fear of the Lord, And He shall not judge by the sight of His eyes, Nor decide by the hearing of His ears;*
4 *But with righteousness He shall judge the poor, And decide with equity for the meek of the earth; **He shall strike the earth with the rod of His mouth, And with the breath of His lips He shall slay the wicked.***

Now obviously the church did not give birth to Christ. Neither did Israel get caught up to heaven. <u>So the identity of the woman should be easy, it has to be **Israel.**</u> The identity of the dragon is no mystery, it is the devil. What I want to point out here is **the anger and hatred the dragon has for the woman**. If you study Israel's history you will see that the devil has tried to destroy them repeatedly thru the years. In Egypt, Babylon, Rome and other places; under the rule of Muhammad and Hitler and other people Israel has had a constant war for its survival.

Millions of Israelis have died because of the fear of the devil and his hatred of Christ. From Eve's sin and the promise of one who would bruise the head of the devil, the devil has tried to stop the plan of God and kill the Christ.

15So the serpent spewed water out of his mouth like a flood after the woman that he might cause her to be carried away by the flood. The fact that the devil spewed water out of his mouth is interesting. **Water is always used of something spiritual**. It is used as a type of the Holy Spirit; as a type of spiritual sanctification.

So it is clear that here the devil is using **spiritual means** to rally his followers to persecute the woman. It is only religion that enables him to keep his hold over the earth. Common sense would kick in if they were not tied to him for religious reasons.

Does the Koran teach its followers to persecute the Jews? Yes in fact it teaches that the Muslim will destroy the Jews and that even rocks and trees will call out, " **oh Muslim, here is a Jew hiding behind me, come and kill him**". The Koran teaches the Muslim to not trust or make friends with either a Christian or a Jew. From childhood they are taught to hate their enemies as the enemies of Allah.

The devil will always try to hide who he is behind a religious mask. It is not in his interest to be honest with anyone. Therefore he will mask his true nature until the end. There is no doubt that the people who will rally against Israel will really believe that it is Gods will for them to kill all Israelis. Normal people don't sit around and fantasize about killing people. Yet millions of Muslims believe that to kill someone for Allah is the only sure way to paradise.

Why else would a Muslim be willing to kill or die?
Muhammads Perverted Paradise

Virgins, boys and wine;

Koran 78:31

as for the righteous, they shall surely triumph. Theirs shall be gardens and vineyards, and high- bosomed virgins for companions: a truly overflowing cup.

Koran 37:40-48

...They will sit with bashful, dark-eyed virgins, as chaste as the sheltered eggs of ostriches.

Al Hadis, Vol. 4, p. 172, No. 34

***Ali reported that the Apostle of Allah said, "There is in Paradise a market wherein there will be no buying or selling, but will* consist of men and women. When a man desires a beauty, he will have intercourse with them."**

There is also wine to drink;

Koran 47:15

Here is a Parable of the Garden which the righteous are promised. In it are...rivers of wine...

Homosexual relationships will be allowed in heaven;

Koran 52:24

Round about them will serve, to them, boys (handsome) as pearls well-guarded.

Koran 56:17

Round about them will serve boys of perpetual freshness.

Koran 76:19

and round about them will serve boys of perpetual freshness: if thou see them, thou wouldst think them scattered pearls.

When a martyr for Allah is killed the first drop of his blood is said to pay the penalty for all sins he may have committed in life. Plus he can then pray for 70 family members and they will have access to paradise. Thus Islam glorifies death over life.

The mount of the congregation

Isaiah 14:13, the mount of the congregation; the name is from the Babylonian religion. It was a mythical mountain that had its top in heaven and its roots go down to the "holy deep". It was called by them, "the mighty mountain of Bel". It was the place that satan claimed would be his launching platform to reach above the stars of God. In this mount, a man could expect to receive any carnal pleasure he desired. Nothing would be off limits to him once he was there. This is the origin of Muhammad's beliefs of paradise.

It is interesting to note the similarities between the tower of Babel and the boast of the devil; both desired to have a united dominion, both intended to reach even unto heaven by means of their labor, and both were confounded in their work by the judgment of God.

Mountains in the Bible signify kingdoms. The seven mountains that the woman sits on in **Revelation 17:9-10 are** seven kings or kingdoms that she rules over. In **Daniel 2:35,** Daniel saw a stone cut without hands that destroyed the image and became a mountain so great that it filled the whole earth, this of course means the kingdom of Christ on earth, **Isaiah 9:6.** That kingdom will have no end.

In **Revelation 17:12** John is told of ten kings who will receive a kingdom for a short period with the antichrist-mahdi. The woman, who is ancient, will have seven kingdoms at her feet that she rules over. I believe that this is the Sunni nations to the south of Babylon.

For the people of the desert regions of the Middle East who worship Allah, there is nothing much in this world to look forward to. Women are little more than cattle. Islam doesn't promise the followers joy in this life at all. Christianity promises the believer joy unspeakable and full of glory. Islam simply says that Allah does what he wants. If he wants to make you have leprosy, well there is nothing you can do about it, its Allah's will.

The promise of a life in eternity where you can do anything you desire is appealing to someone who has only seen sand and dirt their whole life. The lure of sex and carnal gratification is the very thing that Jesus warned us about. He said it would lead to death, Muhammad said it was the reward of faithfulness to Islam.

Christianity; Jesus teaches clearly that all sexual perverts would be cast into the lake of fire as punishment.

Islam; the followers of Muhammad are taught to expect sexual perversion as a reward in heaven. What a clear difference is made. No wonder sinners prefer Islam! Sex is included! The flesh is rewarded!

There is no denying of ourselves in Islam, only an expectation that one day we can be spiritually perverted and that God would still want us in His heaven. **How can a Holy God accept perverts into His house? The answer is that He will not!**

The very things that forced God to destroy the Canaanites are the things that Muhammad promised to his followers. While it may be fashionable to call Islam a great religion, I think the Word of God would disagree.

Verse 17; *the dragon went to make war with the remnant of her seed.* This verse should be understood to be linked to chapter 13.

Revelation 13:1-8

*[1] (RSV) And I saw a beast rising out of the sea, with ten horns and seven heads, with ten diadems upon its horns and a blasphemous name upon its heads. [2] And the beast that I saw was like a leopard, its feet were like a bear's, and its mouth was like a lion's mouth. And to it the dragon gave **his power and his throne and great authority.***

[3] One of its heads seemed to have a mortal wound, but its mortal wound was healed, and the whole earth followed the beast with wonder.

*[4] Men worshiped the dragon, for he had given his authority to the beast, and they worshiped the beast, saying, **"Who is like the beast, and who can fight against it?"*** **(Remember, no one could resist the two prophets, Enoch and Elijah until the beast killed them.** He will be known previous to this, but after the two witnesses are killed he will have miracles and a miracle man on his side. Not only will he have seemingly miraculous power over death, he will do what no one else has been able to do. This proves that miracles will not convince the world. The two witnesses did miracles, but the world did not want to be convinced then any more than they do now. No miracle is greater than a transformed soul. God does real miracles constantly, yet the world ignores them. They don't want God because they want to live in sin.)

[5] and the beast was <u>given a mouth uttering haughty and blasphemous words</u>, and it was allowed to exercise authority for forty-two months; **(3.5 years).**

[6] it opened its mouth to utter blasphemies against God, blaspheming his name and his dwelling, that is, those who dwell in heaven. <u>According to the Apostle John, whoever denies the Son has denied the Father</u>

(1John 2:23). The antichrist Mahdi will deny that God has a Son. Islam is covered in this blasphemy.

⁷*Also it was allowed to make war on the saints and to conquer them* (Saints here means the Jews in Israel). *And authority was given it over every tribe and people and tongue and nation,* (this makes it clear that even after 3.5 years of vivid testimonials from the two witnesses, the world will prefer a man over God.)

⁸ *and all who dwell on earth will worship it, every one whose name has not been written before the foundation of the world in the book of life of the Lamb that was slain.* A religious celebration orchestrated from satan.

Although the antichrist will rule previous to this point, from the middle part of the tribulation he will take on the most sinister characteristics of his god, satan. Although the Muslims count the devil as an enemy, it is clear from their convoluted doctrines that it is the devil that is behind Islam. It is clear that the devil is the reason for the antichrist raising an army to go to Jerusalem to conquer the two prophets.

According to scripture the antichrist will be able to conquer at least a third of the city. God will not allow the Muslims to take the whole city at that time. Today one third of Jerusalem is Muslim, the eastern side. It is easy to see how the antichrist will regain control of one third. The Temple Mount is in the Muslim section.

RETURNING TO THE OLD TESTAMENT PASSAGES CONCERNING ANTICHRIST

In Daniel 7:20 we are told that the antichrist had eyes and a mouth that spoke impressive things. The eyes speak of understanding and wisdom. **Ezekiel 28:3** says that he is wiser than Daniel. There is no secret hidden from him. He will be an impressive figure. Arguments will be useless against him. He will be able to out-speak anyone. No man will have the ability to resist him. His will be a powerful spiritual and satanic personality.

Because the devil will give him his seat and authority the antichrist will take on the exact nature of the devil. His personality will be the human version of satan. **Ezekiel 28:2** says, "Your heart is lifted up and you say, "I am a god; **I sit in god's seat** in the midst of the seas," meaning Jerusalem. One of the first things the antichrist will do after the two witnesses are killed will be to go into the rebuilt temple and defile it probably by putting his statue in it. This is the same image that can speak.

Jesus said this would be the abomination that makes desolate. **Matthew 24:15-16** *"Therefore when you see the 'abomination of desolation,' spoken of by Daniel the prophet, standing in the holy place"* (whoever reads, let him understand), **16***then let those who are in Judea flee to the mountains.* (The area that was Judea is mostly Muslim now, they will have to hide in the Sinai Peninsula to escape his wrath.)

Daniel 7:27 says that he will bring the abomination that makes desolate. **2 Thes. 2:4 who opposes and exalts himself above all that is called God or that is worshiped, so that he sits as God in the temple of God, showing himself that he is God.** Never lose sight of this fact, this is a man. He will have the same vanity that any man will have. He will become convinced of his own superiority.

Rev. 13:8

All who dwell on the earth will worship him, *whose names have not been written in the Book of Life of the Lamb slain from the foundation of the world,*

The antichrist will expect worship, just as the devil demands worship and seeks it. **Only** the ransomed will refuse to worship him. This will result in their deaths.

Shari-a law will be the law of the land under the antichrist. This means that public beheadings and executions will be normal. Muhammad sent his followers to kill anyone who even made a poem he didn't like, the antichrist will have the same spirit of jealousy and hate. He will rule with an iron fist. **Isaiah 14:6** says that he will rule the people with a continual stroke, and will rule the nations in anger.

In **Daniel 7:25** we are told that he will seek to change times and laws. Only a Muslim would want to change laws and times. If you ask a Muslim what year it is, he is not going to count from the birth of Jesus, he is going to count from the conquest of Muhammad. It is their goal to change times to line up to their reckoning.

In **Daniel 7:21** it tells us that he will be able to make war with the Holy People, (the Jews) and overcome them. He will trample the people under his feet for 3.5 years (the last half of the tribulation).

You only have to look at Afghanistan to see what Sharia law is like; soccer stadiums filled with people who have come to watch a beheading. This is what's coming!

What part will the antichrist' partner the false prophet play? He will draw all men to the antichrist and make people worship him and his image which the false prophet **(the Muslim version of Jesus)** will give life to.

The false Jesus

Rev. 13:11-15

*Then I saw another beast coming up out of the earth, and **he had two horns like a lamb and spoke like a dragon.**(The reference here to the lamb is not insignificant; the Lamb of God is Jesus Christ. This beast that arises from the earth is a false Christ. As I have pointed out, the Muslims expect Jesus to come to help the Mahdi kill the two witnesses. A lamb of course does not have horns but this one does. Its horns represent the dragons influence. The devil will give him his ability to speak.)

12*And he exercises all the authority of the first beast in his presence, and causes the earth and those who dwell in it to **worship the first beast,*** (notice here it is the false Christ who causes everyone to worship the antichrist. He plays the part of a servant to his master the Mahdi.) *Whose deadly wound was healed.* ("Healed" this will appear to be a miracle to the world.)

13*He performs great signs, so that he even makes fire come down from heaven on the earth in the sight of men.* (The two witnesses will be known for their miracles. This false prophet Jesus will also be able to perform *miracles*. In **2 Timothy 3:8** Paul tells us about the two men who opposed Moses and Aaron, Jannes and Jambres. According to Exodus 7 these men were able to perform miracles in opposition to God.)

*14And **he deceives** those who dwell on the earth by those signs which he was granted to do in the sight of the beast,* **(2Co 11:13** *for such are false apostles, **deceitful workers,** transforming themselves into the apostles of Christ.*

2Co 11:14 *And no marvel; for Satan himself is transformed into an angel of light).* (It is clear that the false Jesus will convince many that he is **really of God**. Miracles and his preaching will fool the world. Notice how he deceives the people by those signs he was able to do. The world wants **their version of Jesus,** but not the real Jesus.)

Rev.13:14 *Telling those who dwell on the earth to make an image to the beast who **was wounded by the sword and lived** (there is every indication that the antichrist was stricken in battle, or at least appeared to have been, yet he recovered in a seemingly miraculous way.)

Vs 15; *And he had power to **give life** (the word translated as life in the original Greek is the word **"pnuema"** which means spirit, breath or wind. It is not **"Zoe"** in the Greek which indeed does mean life. Therefore it seems likely that this image will have breath, but in reality will not be a living being. It will fool men, but it will be a lie.) *Unto the image of the beast, that the image of the beast should both speak, and cause that as many as would not worship the image of the beast should be killed.* Notice again that it is the false Jesus who is causing people to be killed. The Apostle Paul said that he would perform lying wonders to deceive those who are perishing **(2Thess. 2:9).** It is not the antichrist who is pushing the religious reforms, it is his puppet prophet. He will do what he can to help the Mahdi achieve his goals.

This version of Jesus is nothing like the real Jesus. He will do miracles, but they will be for the purpose of deceiving those who dwell on earth.

We are told in Daniel and again in Revelation that the antichrist will have a deadly wound and that it would be miraculously healed.

Just what type of wound it will be we are not told, but we should take this scripture at face value. **It is clear that a miracle of some sort will restore the antichrist Mahdi to life**.

We do not know for sure what part of the tribulation it will happen in except that the whole world will wonder after the Mahdi with great admiration. I personally feel that this might happen when the mahdi is going to make war against the two witnesses.

If so it will be a great propaganda tool for the devil to use and from scripture it is clear he uses it.

Here we have the false trinity played out on earth. The devil, antichrist and the false prophet are an evil imitation of the truth.

The false prophet will be the one who institutes the new laws on the world. Shari-a law, Muslim rule will be the law. What does Shari-a law mean? **It means that all non-Muslims must either convert or die.** Although the two witnesses will be killed, it is clear that not all of Israel will be conquered. The Muslims will regain the Temple Mount area, but the nation of Israel will still exist. It will be another 3.5 years before antichrist attempts to conquer all of Israel.

Rev. 13:16-18; the mark of the beast

He **(the false prophet, the Muslim Jesus)** *causes all, both small and great, rich and poor, free and slave, to receive a mark on their* **right hand** *or on* **their foreheads,** *[17]and that no one may buy or sell except one who* **has the mark** *or* **the name** *of the beast, or the* **number of his name.** *[18]Here is wisdom. Let him who has understanding calculate the number of the beast, for it is the number of a man: His number is 666.*

The false Jesus is the one who institutes Muslim rule. He will use economic laws to enforce conversion to Islam. Every faithful follower of Islam will receive a mark. There are actually three things spoken of by John here. They are the **MARK,** the **NAME,** and the **NUMBER OF THE NAME.**

People will not receive the number 666 on their hands or foreheads. That is not what the bible says at all. What it does say is that the people will receive the mark or else they will not eat or buy or sell. And what is the mark? There exists a technology called RFID (radio frequency I.D). It is a microchip which stores important information and can be scanned, and can be placed in a card. It is the size of a grain of rice. The card is in use today in a variety of ways. Mobile one speed pass uses this technology. It also can be tracked via global positioning satellites.

It is also used to keep track of pets, new cars, and is used in smart cards. There also is an advance model of this chip which can be recharged by changes in temperature. Over one and a half million dollars was spent to find out that the two places in the body that the temperature changes the most rapidly. They are in the **FOREHEAD**, and on the **BACK OF THE HAND.**

Think about it, they will know who and where every person is and to get food it will take **conversion to Islam.** Once again I want to emphasize it; this is all spiritual and not political. The reason for the development of the mark in our day may be financial but the reason in the tribulation will be conversion pure and simple.

To take the mark then will be the same as denying Christ. If anyone will deny Jesus, Jesus said he will deny them. **Matthew 10:33** *but whoever denies Me before men, him I will also deny before My Father who is in heaven.* To receive food a person must show allegiance to Islam and the antichrist Mahdi. How many hungry people will say the words and accept the forced conversion by receiving the mark? Apparently many millions will. What then is the name of the beast?

IDENTIFYING THE NAME OF THE BEAST: Χξς =666?

The letters above represent what John saw and the exact order that he put them in the Revelation in Ch. 13:18. They are pronounced "**Chi, Ksee, Sigma**". Now I know this will mess you up a bit, but even though these are Greek letters, they also read in Arabic, the language of Islam. Greek reads from left to right. Arabic reads from right to left, the same as Hebrew. Ex Muslim terrorist, now a Christian, Walid Shoebat said that he was startled to see the Greek letters χξς' translated as "666" in **Revelation 13:18.** He said that if one draws these same letters as if they were Arabic letters, (R-L) the ξς' are identical to Arabic letters for "**Bism Allah**" that translates into English as "in the **name** of **Allah!** The χ becomes the crossed swords of Islam.

The name of the beast is what John said, one who comes in the **name of Allah**. Allah is the beast name. Who then is the beast? It can be none other than the Mahdi.

Notice also that not everyone receives the mark. Some have the name, some the number of his name. **Rev 13:17** And that no man might buy or sell, 1.save he that had the mark, 2. Or the name of the beast. 3. or the number of his name.

There are 99 names of Allah. Here is a partial list. The humiliator, The subtle one, The highest and sublime, The causer of death, The taker of life, The hidden one, The creator of the harmful, The distresser, The patient one, The proud one, The afflicter, The great plotter, A floating star, The great deceiver, Lord of the dawn, king of multitudes and demons.

If you are a student of the Bible these names should sound somewhat familiar, they are **Biblical descriptions of the devil**.

The name of the beast is "Allah". The devil gave him his power, his throne, and his ability. If a man can convince the 1.5 billion Muslims to follow him as Caliph he will have enormous power.

Do Muslims wear the name of the beast? In a word, yes! The badge of servitude that the jihadists wear over their foreheads is the name of Allah. It seems that only those new converts or those who are forced to convert will need to receive a chip implant because the followers of the Mahdi will already have the name.

144,000

Notice the next scene we are shown; the 144,000 followers of the Lamb are now in heaven. <u>Rev. 14:1-5</u>

*Then I looked, and behold, a Lamb standing on Mount Zion, and with Him one hundred and forty-four thousand, having His Father's name written on their foreheads. 2And I heard a voice from heaven, like the voice of many waters, and like the voice of loud thunder. And I heard the sound of harpists playing their harps. 3They sang as it were a new song before the throne, before the four living creatures, and the elders; and no one could learn that song except the hundred and forty-four thousand who were redeemed from the earth. 4These are the ones who were not defiled with women, for they are virgins. **<u>These are the ones who follow the Lamb wherever He goes</u>**. These were redeemed from among men, being first fruits to God and to the Lamb. 5And in their mouth was found no deceit, for they are without fault before the throne of God.*

They were redeemed from every tribe of Israel, but they are Messianic Israelites, for they follow the Lamb. This is why I believe that the antichrist kills them. To accept his mark is to deny Jesus Christ. Not the false Christ who worships the mahdi antichrist, but the real Lamb of God. **<u>We are told that the antichrist will rule in Jerusalem for 3.5 years.</u>** This is the time of Great Tribulation. They are seen in Heaven here. They were first seen on the earth, but are now in Heaven. This makes it sound very much as if they have died for Christ and the Word of their testimonies.

Chapter ten

The Coming Flood Of Martyrdom

In **Chapter 14:9-13** we are told that many, many people would die for refusing to receive the mark of the beast. In fact it is such a harvest of souls that we are shown one like the Son of Man (Jesus) reaping the enormous harvest. In **Chapter 15:2-4** we are again shown the redeemed who gave their lives rather than receive the mark. Obviously there will be many who will choose death over conversion. **Rev. 14:20** _And the winepress was trampled **outside the city,** and blood came out of the winepress, up to the horses' bridles,_(about six feet deep) _for one thousand six hundred furlongs._ About 200 miles long, Israel's eastern border is just over 250 miles long.

Because so many are beheaded some prophecy teachers have concluded that the church hasn't been raptured at this point in the tribulation. I don't believe that that is the answer at all. Rather I see it as proof that the two witnesses have converted many to believe the Gospel. The 144,000 will have been missionaries to the world and God will help them to preach the word. **Dan 11:33** _And those who understand among the people shall teach many._ Many will believe their word. Not all of mankind will follow the beast.

Rev. 15:1-8 &16:1-21

Then I saw another sign in heaven, great and marvelous: **seven angels having the seven last plagues, for in them the wrath of God is complete.** **Rev. 15:5-8** After these things I looked, and behold, the temple of the tabernacle of the testimony in heaven was opened. ⁶And out of the temple came the seven angels having the seven plagues, clothed in pure bright linen, and having their chests girded with golden bands. ⁷Then one of the four living creatures gave to the **seven angels' seven golden bowls full of the wrath of God** who lives forever and ever.

The Seven Vial Plagues Are Poured Out

FIRST PLAGUE; a noisome and grievous sore came upon the people who had the mark.

SECOND PLAGUE; every living thing in the sea died because the sea became as the blood of a dead man.

THIRD PLAGUE; all fresh water is stricken and also becomes blood

FOURTH PLAGUE; the heat of the sun is increased until men are scorched by the heat

FIFTH PLAGUE; darkness upon the seat of the beast kingdom until they gnawed their tongues for pain

SIXTH PLAGUE; water is dried up until the river Euphrates is dried up

SEVENTH PLAGUE; IT IS DONE! Mighty earthquake destroys 1/3rd of the city of Jerusalem (Muslim portion?) and great hailstones weighing about 100 lbs each fall on people killing many.

The Final Solution; Armageddon

Revelation 16:13-14

13 (RSV) And I saw, issuing from the mouth of the dragon and from the mouth of the beast and from the mouth of the false prophet, three foul spirits like frogs;

*14 for they are **demonic spirits, performing signs,** who go abroad to the kings of the whole world, to assemble them for battle on the great day of God the Almighty.*

Once again we see spiritual beings involved in the end-times work of the devil and the antichrist and the false prophet. **The spirits like frogs come out of their mouths.** Remember it is the devil who gave the antichrist mahdi the ability to speak as he does. The second beast, the false Jesus, also speaks as the mahdi. Both of these have demonic abilities to influence people to do what they say.

Rev. 16:16

The spirits gathered the kings at the place which is called Armageddon in Hebrew.

And what do they seek for people to do? To gather them together to make war against Israel. One final solution, just like Hitler before him. It is in the Koran that the Muslims will eventually destroy the Jews. It will take very little to convince the average Muslim to attack Israel. The kings of the earth and of the whole world will join in the attack. Antichrist will have the world system at his disposal and he will use it.

Chapter eleven

Revelation 17:1-6. The Great Prostitute.
¹ (ASV) and there came one of the seven angels that had the seven bowls, and spoke with me, saying, Come hither, I will show thee **the judgment of the great harlot that sitteth upon many waters;** (the waters represent people. She literally is in many different nations. **NOTICE; SHE IS DESCRIBED AS A PROSTITUTE.**)
² with whom the kings of the earth committed fornication and they that dwell in the earth were made drunken with the wine of her fornication. (However innocently they may present it; playing games with the devil will eventually cost them their souls. They partook of her. She is in the wilderness, that is, the desert area.)
³ And he carried me away in the Spirit into a wilderness: and I saw a woman sitting upon **a scarlet-colored beast,** *full of names of blasphemy, having seven heads and ten horns.* **The antichrist carries the woman.** She existed before this, but is propelled forward by the beast. There is no doubt that the antichrist uses her to further his goals. The woman represents a religious system. She gladly hops on the antichrist to get where she thinks he will take her. In Islam today there is an eager expectation of what the Mahdi will do once he takes power.
I believe that based on scripture most Muslims will not suspect his true intent is to deceive and to destroy even the religion he is supposed to promote. He is like satan, for he gets his power and authority from satan. As the devil seeks to steal, kill and to destroy so will his hand picked man.

Notice something about the antichrist Mahdi as John describes him; he is scarlet colored. That means he is the color of blood. What a fitting description of the man. He will literally bring blood and death to the world in the name of deliverance and true religion! The Bible says that the ten horns are ten kings that will rule one hour with the beast and that they will hate the woman. Islam will think that the deliverer has come, but he will be the destroyer instead.

⁴ And the woman was arrayed in purple and scarlet, and decked with gold and precious stone and pearls, having in her hand a golden cup full of abominations, even the unclean things of her fornication, (her real image is revolting. Purple and scarlet are royal and holy colors, meaning she is ruling as a religious organization. The religion in the desert (wilderness) can only be Islam.)

⁵ And upon her forehead a name written, MYSTERY, BABYLON THE GREAT, THE MOTHER OF THE HARLOTS AND OF THE ABOMINATIONS OF THE EARTH. ⁶ And I saw the woman drunken with the blood of the saints, and with the blood of the martyrs (martyrs in Greek means witnesses) *of Jesus. And when I saw her, I wondered with a great wonder.* We have to ask, "How many more dead Christians will Islam demand? For every insult they perceive they demand more. The Pope insults Islam so they kill innocent people that have nothing at all to do with the Pope. The woman was extremely drunk with the Christians blood. This means she never stopped or got tired of their blood. It also is clear that during the tribulation this religious system will be responsible for the deaths of millions of witnesses.

The great mystery; Babylon the religious system.

First we must understand that the antichrist uses the religious system to gain power. Therefore it is Islam which is the great whore. She is drunk with the blood of saints and martyrs of Jesus. This is shown to John immediately after the antichrist takes over the Temple Mount area.

It is clear that the antichrist mahdi and the false Jesus persecute the believers by the millions. Blood will flow **Rev. 14:20** *And the winepress was trampled outside the city, and blood came out of the winepress, up to the horses' bridles, for one thousand six hundred furlongs.*

Islam has blood on its hands to answer for. The God of Justice will requite their bloody deeds the same way He did Cain's. For 1400 years Muslims have killed to further their religion; all the while claiming that it was God who told them to. The first murder was caused over religion. Cain killed Abel because Abel offered a better sacrifice to God than Cain did. Religion in the name of any God that kills is religion in the person of the devil.

The inquisitions of the dark ages don't begin to compare with the deeds of the so-called religion of peace. Islam is submission, either you submit or die. Blood shed is no problem to a Muslim. As much as we are excited by the last chance the world will get thru the two witnesses, we should warn people of the terrible price that will be paid to be Christians. Many will die and many more will renounce their faith out of fear of death. This will cause the father to turn against the children as Jesus predicted.

Muhammad is quoted in the Hadith as saying, "The sword is the key of heaven and hell. A **drop of blood** in the cause of Allah — a night spent in arms (war) — is of **more avail than two months of fasting and prayer**. Whosoever falls in battle, his sins are forgiven, and at the Day of Judgment, his limbs shall be supplied by the wings of angels and cherubim."

From its inception, Islam has been committed to what it calls **jihad**, a word meaning holy war or inner struggle. The duty of Muslims is to subjugate or destroy "infidels", the term the Koran uses for all non-believers. From the Muslim viewpoint, the world is divided into two regions — those areas controlled by Islam, called Dar al-Islam (meaning the House of Islam) and those called Dar al-Harb (the House of War). The Koran commands Muslims to fight non-Muslims until they exterminate all other religions, leaving Islam as the one and only religion in the world (Suras 2:193 and 8:39). Muhammad is also quoted in the Hadith as saying, **"I have been ordered to fight with the people until they say; none has the right to be worshiped but Allah" (Hadith 4:196).**

Regarding terror, Allah orders Muslims to terrorize non-Muslims on his behalf: **"Strike terror (into the hearts of) the enemies of Allah and your enemies" (Sura 8:60).** Allah then assures his followers that he will assist them: **"I will instill TERROR into the hearts of unbelievers. Smite them above their necks (cut off their heads) and smite all their finger tips off them. It is not you who slays them. It is Allah"** Sura 8:12&17.

Concerning jihad, the Koran guarantees Paradise to those who fight for Allah (Sura 4:74). It promises instant Paradise for those who die in battle (Suras 9:111 and 47:5-6).

Dying for Allah is presented as better than living: **"And if you are killed or die in the Way of Allah, forgiveness and mercy from Allah are far better than all that others may amass"** (Sura 3:157)

The following are the guiding principles of Islam. No where do we find love and forgiveness. Read just a few quotes from Muhammad; and see if they don't remind you of Assyria the bloody empire.

"Fighting is prescribed for you and (some of) you dislike it. But it is possible that you dislike a thing which is good for you, and that you love a thing which is bad for you. **But Allah knows, and you know not"** (Sura 2:216).

"Fight and slay the pagans wherever you find them, beleaguer them, and lie in wait for them in every stratagem of war" (Sura 9:5).

"Fight in the way of Allah . . . and slay them (the unbelievers) wherever you find them and drive them out; and fight them until all religion is for Allah" (Sura 2:190-193).

This religion will give the antichrist the platform to rise up, yet according to scripture he and his puppet kings will make war on the religious system and destroy it. **Rev. 17:16-18** *And the ten horns which you saw on the beast,* **these will hate the harlot, make her desolate and naked, eat her flesh and burn her with fire.** (The ten kings destroy the woman, which is later described as Babylon.) *17For God has put it into their hearts to fulfill His purpose, to be of one mind, and to give their kingdom to the beast, until the words of God are fulfilled. 18And the woman whom you saw is that great city which reigns over the kings of the earth."*

It is clear that the antichrist makes war on the religion that he used to gain power. That could mean that he will purge Islam. That is one of the things that the Mahdi is prophesied to do.

It may be that he attacks the Sunni's or anyone who doesn't fit his version of what a good Muslim should be.

Why would the antichrist destroy modern Islam? Because **he will make a new Islam,** one centered on worship to him. The question then arises whether or not Muslims kill each other over religious disagreements. Actually they have been killing each other as long as they have existed. Sunni Muslims consider the Shiites and all other branches of Islam to be infidels. No two branches get along for long. The only time they cooperate is when the end justifies the means.

The Identification Of The Great City; Babylon

Next we are shown a city where the woman sits. She reigns from the city over all people on earth. At the time the book of Revelation was written there was only one city on earth that fit that description and that was Rome. However, today Rome does not even come close to fitting the description given of this city.

There is only one city that all Muslims look to; **Mecca**. It is from this city that the religion of Islam started. This was Muhammad's home town. Yet it was in Babylon and the surrounding regions the worship of the moon god originated with its symbol as the crescent moon. In the book of Judges chapter 8:21 we read where Gideon killed the leaders of Midian and took their ornaments off of their camels necks. The word translated "ornaments" is "Saharan" in Hebrew. It means moon ornaments. These were worshippers of the moon.

Sin, the original name of Allah.

It was in Ur of the Chaldees that Abraham was called by Jehovah God to leave his family and his families' gods. The national god of Babylon and Ur was the moon god known as Sin. His symbol was the crescent moon. Where did the worship of Allah come from? Actually it came from Babylon long before Muhammad came along. **The crescent moon symbol of Islam is a remnant of ancient pagan moon worship.**

Muhammad grew up worshipping many pagan gods in the Kabah including the moon, either called <u>Hubal</u> and <u>Allah</u>. After his conversion to monotheism, through the influence of Christians, Muhammad stopped worshiping the moon. The same is true for all Muslims since, down to the present day. However, the crescent moon is the universal symbol of Islam. Muslims will argue that there is no archeological evidence for the crescent moon symbol being used in Islam for the first few centuries after Muhammad. There is actually much evidence that it was.

The Muslims also claim that Koran in its completed form existed in the time of Muhammad, yet there is no archeological evidence for this claim. What we can be sure of, is the moon worship was more prevalent in Arabia than any other part of the world and that the symbol of the crescent moon has been used by the **Arab religions as far back as the time of Abraham.**

It is a falsification of history to think there is no connection with the history of the crescent moon symbol of pagan moon god worship and Islam. The fact remains that most Arab/Muslim countries today still use the crescent moon symbol on their flags and atop of their mosques. The connection is so powerful that only the blind would reject any connection.

The Babylonians had a different name for Allah; they called him by the name **Sin**, where we get our word for sin.

"Sin.—the moon-god occupied the chief place in the astral triad. Its other two members, Shamash the sun and Ishtar the planet Venus, were his children. Thus it was, in effect, from the night that light had emerged....In his physical aspect Sin—who was venerated at Ur under the name of Nannar—was an old man with along beard the color of lapis-lazuli.

He normally wore a turban. Every evening he got into his barque— which to mortals appeared in the form of a brilliant crescent moon—and navigated the vast spaces of the nocturnal sky. Some people, however, believed that the luminous crescent was Sin's weapon.

But one day the crescent gave way to a disk which stood out in the sky like a gleaming crown. There could be no doubt that this was the god's own crown; and then Sin was called "Lord of the Diadem". These successive and regular transformations lent Sin a certain mystery. For this reason he was considered to be **'He whose deep heart no god can penetrate'**... Sin was also full of wisdom.

At the end of every month the gods came to consult them and he made decisions for them...His wife was Ningal, 'the great Lady'. He was the father not only of Shamash and Ishtar but also of a son Nusku, the god fire." (Larousse Encyclopedia of Mythology, 1960, p 54-56)

Muhammad describes Allah as one whom no man can know because he is too deep for man. Sounds very similar to the Babylonian description of Sin.

Contrary to Muslim claims the worship of the Moon god Sin was common and widespread in the homeland of Abraham. God told Abraham to leave the land and gods of his fathers and come to a land that Jehovah would show him. Ur is near Babylon and home to Moon worship.

Although Muslims do not worship the moon or idols, their pagan origins influenced Muhammad in his legislation concerning how and where to worship Allah. Originally Allah was only one of over 360 idols in the Kabah of Mecca. Muhammad eventually destroyed all but the one to Allah and Allah's three daughters. Later he destroyed the daughter worship too. This is where he admitted that it was satan who had inspired him to allow it.

This is the so-called satanic verses.

"Do you see Al lat and Al Uzza, and Manat the third idol besides? They are the Sublime Birds, and their intercession is desirable indeed!"

These were the names of Allah's daughters. This passage has been a source of embarrassment for Muslims for years. Muhammad admitted that it was the devil who spoke thru him on this occasion.

Tabari 6:110, "when Muhammad brought a revelation from Allah canceling what satan had cast on the tongue of his prophet, the Quraysh said, 'Muhammad has repented of what he said concerning the position of our gods with Allah."

So we see that according to Muhammad, some of the time he couldn't tell the devil from God.

Why does the bible call this great city Babylon? Look at the original Babylon. It was the center for every false teaching that has spread across the earth. It was Babylon that gave rise to the entire pantheon of gods that infiltrated Greece, Rome, Egypt and the entire Mediterranean world. The devil used this religious system to corrupt the truth.

WHAT HAPPENS TO THE CITY?

In one hour she is destroyed. The fact that people stand afar off for fear of her torments would make you believe that it is a nuclear attack that destroys Mecca. **Rev. 18:8-11**

*Therefore her plagues will come in one day--death and mourning and famine. **And she will be utterly burned with fire**, for strong is the Lord God who judges her.*

*9"The kings of the earth who committed fornication and lived luxuriously with her will weep and lament for her, **when they see the smoke of her burning,** 10standing at a distance for fear of her torment, saying, 'Alas, alas, that great city Babylon, that mighty city! **For in one hour your judgment has come.'** 11And the merchants of the earth will weep and mourn over her, for no one buys their merchandise anymore:*

Something to keep in mind here, **the kings and the beast destroy the woman.** It doesn't say the people will know this though. It seems that the people will see Israel as the perpetrator of the attack. **Dan 11:44** *Then he will go out with great fury to destroy, and to devote many to destruction.* He will destroy his own as Isaiah said.

The devil and the false prophet and the antichrist have already sent out the spirits like frogs to gather everyone together against Israel, **Rev. 16:13-14**. All they will need is a provocation. The wiping out of Mecca would certainly do. Why would the antichrist destroy Mecca? **Because the New Islam will be based in Jerusalem.** Also Muhammad is said to have predicted that the city would be destroyed. I believe that the devil will seek to find a reason to destroy Israel and this will be it.

Examine some of the clues that God gives in chapter 18 about Babylon.

1. <u>The nations committed fornication with her.</u> Today almost every nation on earth is compromising with Islam to get favor and oil. The power of oil has caused Europe and Asia to bend to the Muslim whip. America's colleges are allowing pro-Islamic teaching to be taught in the universities because Saudi Arabia is giving them money. They are subverting our children and the university leaders are complicit.

2. <u>The merchants of the Earth have gained financially from their relationship with her.</u> Needless to say the financial system we in America rely on is not solid. But what most people don't know is that it is not based on either gold or cash reserves.

   It is actually based on oil. If oil were to drop to $20.00 per barrel it would not be good for America's economy. We are subservient to the Muslim economy whether we admit it or not. Our economy is dependant on theirs.

3. <u>It had slaves in it.</u> In Islam we find the slave trade still alive and flourishing.
4. <u>In verse 19 the Bible says the ships of the sea brought her wealth to nations across the sea.</u> Only oil carries wealth across the sea. Money is transmitted electronically.
5. In her was found the blood of everyone who was slain on the earth. This does not mean ever one who has ever died. It means every one who dies during its reign.

It is clear that the destruction of Babylon will cause all nations to come against Israel, **so it seems likely that all nations will blame Israel for the destruction.**

The final battle will be much like Hitler's final solution in that it will be for the world-wide extinction of the Jewish people. Hitler blamed the Jews for everything that happened and the modern day Muslims are doing the same exact thing. Hate and revenge will motivate them to come up from all over the planet with one thing in mind, kill the Jews.

<u>Israel will not be completely conquered when the antichrist-mahdi and the false Jesus kill the two prophets.</u> The Bible says one-third of the city will be taken. The nation of Israel will still be sovereign and in possession of a mighty army, just as they are now. Remember that Israel has nuclear weapons. No nation can hope to bomb them without suffering the consequences of a nuclear attack.

I think the parallels to Germany in 1938 are remarkable. On November 9-10th the German government organized massive protest against the Jews in Germany, Austria and Czechoslovakia. This was in response to a Jewish youth's killing of a German diplomat in Paris. From this point on all Jewish property was seized by the Nazi's. Innocent people were systematically killed and blamed for all the nations' ills. The dark night became known in history as "Crystal Night", the night of broken glass.

Hitler himself was part Jew. This is a secret that he did not want the world to know. He hated his own. Why? It wasn't him as much as it was the demon spirit behind him. The true spirit of antichrist was behind everything he did just as it will be behind the genuine antichrist. With one exception, the devil himself will empower the future ruler. Even Hitler didn't have that.

The real reason that the Jewish people have been hated is envy. No matter what country they are in, they excel. God has kept His word to Abraham; his seed is exceedingly blessed. This is obvious to anyone who will honestly look. But envy has blinded the eyes of the Muslims. They can't stand the fact that 6 million Jews can succeed without any natural resources to speak of, and the Arabs have failing economies despite having all the oil.

Chapter twelve

The battle of Armageddon, Israel's Last War

In chapter 16 we saw evil spirits like frogs going out to deceive the whole world. Their purpose was to gather all nations to come to Israel for the war to end all wars, Armageddon. It seems that the destruction of Babylon will be used as a means to rally the enemies of Israel together. **Eze 38:10** *Thus saith the Lord Jehovah: It shall come to pass in that day,* ***that things shall come into thy mind, and thou shall devise an evil device***. Their hatred and the influence of the devil will cause them to flock together with a vengeance unparalleled in history. Even Hitler will not compare to the unbridled anger that will exist in their hearts. It is clear that they blame Israel for something. I believe that they will believe that Israel destroyed their holy city Mecca. According to **Daniel 12:11-12**, there are 45 days from the start of the war until it is finished. This means that the battle of Armageddon may last for a month and a half.

The antichrist Mahdi and the false Jesus will rally all true Muslims around the world to come to Israel to destroy the Jews once and for all. Many of the peoples of the world will die before this time and the antichrist will kill many millions more, yet there are still millions who will come. The nations of the old Soviet empire will come as well as Pakistan, Afghanistan, and the Muslims around the world will come. There is no doubt that this will take weeks or even months to organize. As the storm is gathering the nation of Israel will be praying. In Israel today and Judaism in general there are more atheist than believers.

I think when they are faced with extinction they will pray. There are no atheists in hell and there will not be any at Armageddon. As the millions of enemy troops spill over the Litani River into the great valley Israel will be virtually helpless. Only a nuclear bomb could stop them and that would also destroy Israel.

Zec 14:2 *And I will gather all nations to Jerusalem to battle, and **the city shall be taken**, and the houses shall be rifled, and the women shall be* *defiled:* **and half of the city shall go forth into captivity,** *and the rest of the people shall not be taken away out of the city.*

The city of Jerusalem will be retaken by the Muslims. This makes it clear that not all of their armies are in the valley of Megiddo. Gaza and the West Bank will rise up and attack Israel too. When the Bible says half the city will go forth into captivity it makes it clear that the battle will last longer than one or two days. This war may last several days or even a few weeks.

As the Israeli armies are overrun by millions of fanatical Muslims the hope of deliverance will be taken away. The Israeli nation has long held out hope that the Messiah would some day come. Yet they will know that this war will leave no Jew alive. Desperation and fear will be their strength.

Mic 5:5 *and this will be our peace: when the Assyrian comes into our country and his feet are in our land, then we will put up against him* **seven keepers of the flocks and eight chiefs among men.** The nation will not go down without great acts of heroism but they will only slow the Muslim armies down. There will simply be too many. How could the enemy gain the advantage so easily? Because he is already at the gates. Israel is mixed among the Palestinians. There are many excellent Old Testament passages concerning the battle of Armageddon, I want to examine them here.

Joel 1:6-15

6 *(ASV)* **For a nation is come up upon my land, strong, and without number; his teeth are the teeth of a lion, and he hath the jaw-teeth of a lioness.**

7 He hath laid my vine waste, and barked my fig-tree: he hath made it clean bare, and cast it away; the branches thereof are made white. (The fig and vine are both used in the Old Testament to identify Israel).

8 Lament like a virgin girded with sackcloth for the husband of her youth.

9 The meal-offering and the drink-offering are cut off from the **house of Jehovah;** *the priests, Jehovah's ministers, mourn.*

10 The field is laid waste, the land mourneth; for the grain is destroyed, the new wine is dried up, **the oil languisheth.**

15 Alas for the day! For the day of Jehovah is at hand and as destruction from the Almighty shall it come.

141

Rev. Derek Craig Jones

Ezekiel 38:8-16

⁸ *(ASV)* *After many days thou shalt be visited: in the latter years thou shalt come into the land that is brought back from the sword,* **_that is gathered out of many peoples,_** *upon the mountains of Israel, which have been a continual waste; but it is brought forth out of the peoples, and they shall dwell securely, all of them.* **(This is such a fitting picture of modern Israel, literally gathered out of all nations).**

⁹ *And thou shalt ascend, thou shalt come like a storm, thou shalt be like a cloud to cover the land, thou, and all thy hordes, and many peoples with thee.*

¹⁰ *Thus saith the Lord Jehovah: It shall come to pass in that day, that things shall come into thy mind, and* **_thou shalt devise an evil device:_** **(From the devil).**

¹¹ *and thou shalt say, I will go up to the land of unwalled villages; I will go to them that are at rest, that dwell securely, all of them dwelling without walls, and having neither bars nor gates;*

¹² **_to take the spoil and to take the prey; to turn thy hand against the waste places that are now inhabited, and against the people that are gathered out of the nations, that have gotten cattle and goods, that dwell in the middle of the earth._**

¹³ *Sheba, and Dedan, and the merchants of Tarshish, with all the young lions thereof, shall say unto thee, Art thou come to take the spoil? Hast thou assembled thy company to take the prey? To carry away silver and gold, to take away cattle and goods, to take great spoil?*

¹⁴ *Therefore, son of man, prophesy, and say unto Gog, Thus saith the Lord Jehovah:* **_In that day when my people Israel dwelleth securely, shalt thou not know it?_**

¹⁵ **_And thou shalt come from thy place out of the uttermost parts of the north,_** *thou, and many peoples with thee, all of them riding upon horses, a great company and a mighty army;* **(Many of the old Soviet nations are Muslim).**

¹⁶ *and thou shalt come up against my people Israel, as a cloud to cover the land:* **_it shall come to pass in the latter days, that I will bring thee against my land,_**

Ezekiel 39:1-8 *(ASV)* *And thou, son of man, prophesy against Gog, and say, Thus saith the Lord Jehovah: Behold, I am against thee, O Gog, prince of*

Rosh, Meshech, and Tubal: (**Contrary to popular teaching the land of Rosh is not an ancient name for Russia. It was a well known place in Asia Minor. The other places named refer to the peoples of the north. I believe it has more to do with the Islamic nations north and east of Iran.**)

² and I will turn thee about, and will lead thee on, *and will cause thee to come up from the uttermost parts of the north; and I will bring thee upon the mountains of Israel;* (**Here God** says that it is He that will make them to come fight against Israel. You will remember that it was the devil, the antichrist and the false prophet that had spirits like frogs come out of them. Even though the devil had it in his mind to do this, it was God in charge the whole time.**)

³ and I will smite thy bow out of thy left hand, and will cause thine arrows to fall out of thy right hand. (**No weapon formed against us shall prosper! The enemy will be helpless against Jesus and His saints.**)

⁴ Thou shall fall upon the mountains of Israel, thou, and all thy hordes, and the peoples that are with thee: *I will give thee unto the ravenous birds of every sort, and to the beasts of the field to be devoured.* (**Here again the birds are mentioned as in the battle of Armageddon, proving again that this is talking about the same battle.**)

⁵ Thou shall fall upon the open field; for I have spoken it, says the Lord Jehovah.

⁶ And I will send a fire on Magog and on them that dwell securely in the isles; and they shall know that I am Jehovah. Here God speaks of the punishment that is coming on the nations who supported the antichrist. It will reach even unto their homelands.

⁷ And my holy name will I make known in the midst of my people Israel; neither will I suffer my holy name to be profaned any more: and the nations shall know that I am Jehovah, the Holy One in Israel. (**God will sanctify His Name, so it has to be the battle of Armageddon He is speaking about. Although most teachers say this passage talks about a war at the beginning of the tribulation, it is obvious that it is not.**)

⁸ Behold, it cometh, and it shall be done, ***says the Lord Jehovah; this is the day whereof I have spoken.***

God will cause the armies of the earth to come up against Israel so that He may be glorified in them. All the world will assemble together to wipe out what is left of Israel. As millions upon millions of soldiers pour into the valley of Megiddo, others will be attacking from the south and east of Israel. The hope of the nation will be virtually extinguished. The people of Israel will receive no pity from their Muslim conquerors. This is because for their entire lives the Muslims have been taught to hate the Jews. From childhood they were told that the Jews were evil and that to kill them made Allah happy.

The thought that their god would actually want them covered in the blood of the Jews should make them realize that they do not serve the God of the Bible. Jesus was a Jew. The false Jesus will be beside his puppet master the Mahdi as they lead their armies to war. So the battle of Armageddon will finally determine which Jesus will rule; the false prophet or Jesus of the Bible. Remember that Islam teaches that Jesus was a prophet that is why the false Jesus is called the false prophet in Revelation.

And then suddenly, **Jesus and the armies of Heaven** split the eastern sky! **Revelation 19:11-21**

11 (ASV) And I saw the heaven opened; and behold, a white horse, and he that sat thereon called **Faithful and True***; and in righteous he doth judge and make war.* **(Jesus is here presented as the true conqueror, not like the rider on the white horse in chapter six.)**

12 And his eyes are a flame of fire, and upon his head are many diadems; and he hath a name written which no one knoweth but He himself.

*13 And he is arrayed in a garment sprinkled with blood :***(Isaiah 63)** *and his name is called* **The Word of God. (John 1:1)**

14 and the armies which are in heaven followed him upon white horses, clothed in fine linen, white and pure. **(This is a heavenly army made up of the redeemed saints of all the ages.)**

15 And out of his mouth proceeds a sharp sword, that with it he should smite the nations: and he shall rule them with a rod of iron: and he treads the winepress of the fierceness of the wrath of God, the Almighty. **(See Isaiah 63:1-3)**

16 and he hath on his garment and on his thigh a name written, **KINGS OF KINGS, AND LORD OF LORDS. (Jesus at last takes physical control of the Heavens and the Earth)**

Zec 14:4 *And his feet shall stand in that day upon the mount of Olives, which is before Jerusalem on the east; and the mount of Olives shall be* *cleft in the midst thereof toward the east and toward the west, and there shall be a very great valley; and half of the mountain shall remove toward the north, and half of it toward the south.* (When Jesus returns He will come directly to Jerusalem from the valley of Megiddo where He will plant His feet on the Mount of Olives which is just east of the city. The garden of Gethsemane was at the base of the mountain. The mountain will split in two, forming a great valley.)

Zec 14:5 *And ye shall flee by the valley of my mountains; for the valley of the mountains shall reach unto Azel; yea, ye shall flee, like as ye fled from before the earthquake in the days of Uzziah king of Judah; and **Jehovah my God shall come,** and all the holy ones with thee.* (Here Jesus is called **"Jehovah My God"**, proving His divinity. The remnant of Israel will recognize Him as their long awaited Messiah and flee to Him.) **Zec 14:6** *and it shall come to pass in that day, that there shall not be light; the bright ones shall withdraw themselves:*

Zec 14:7 *but it shall be one day which is known unto Jehovah; not day, and not night; but it shall come to pass, that at evening time there shall be light.*

Revelation 19: *[17]And I saw an angel standing in the sun; and he cried with a loud voice, **saying to all the birds that fly in mid heaven,** Come and be gathered together unto the great supper of God; [18] **that ye may eat the flesh of kings,** and the flesh of captains, and the flesh of mighty men, and the flesh of horses and of them that sit thereon, and the flesh of all men, both free and bond, and small and great.*

Zec 14:12 *and this shall be the plague wherewith Jehovah will smite all the peoples that have warred against Jerusalem: **their flesh shall consume away while they stand upon their feet,** and their eyes shall consume away in their sockets, and their tongue shall consume away in their mouth.* (A nuclear blast would disintegrate people; it wouldn't do what Zechariah describes. This is what the sword of Jesus will do to the antichrist' armies.)

Zech. 12:2-3 *"I am going to make Jerusalem a cup that sends all the surrounding peoples reeling. Judah will be besieged as well as Jerusalem. [3]On that day, when all the nations of the earth are gathered against her, I will make Jerusalem an immovable rock for all the nations. All who try to move it will injure themselves.*

145

Eze 39:17 *And thou, son of man, thus saith the Lord GOD:* **Speak unto the birds of every sort,** *and to every beast of the field: Assemble yourselves, and come; gather yourselves on every side to My feast that I do prepare for you, even a great feast, upon the mountains of Israel,* **that ye may eat flesh and drink blood.** (This is repeated in **Revelation 19:17** at the war of Armageddon, proving this is the same battle.)

Eze 39:18 *The flesh of the mighty shall ye eat, and the blood of the princes of the earth shall ye drink; rams, lambs, and goats, bullocks, fatlings of Bashan are they all of them.*

Eze 39:19 *and ye shall eat fat till ye are full and drink blood till ye are drunk, of My feast which I have prepared for you.*

Eze 39:20 *and ye shall be filled at My table with horses and horsemen, with mighty men, and with all men of war, saith the Lord GOD.* (This is quoted almost exactly word for word in the **Revelation 19:17-18**. This should make us see that **the war of Gog and Magog is at the end of time**, just as God told Ezekiel.)

Joel 2:1-11

[1] (ASV) *Blow ye the trumpet in Zion, and sound an alarm in my holy mountain; let all the inhabitants of the land tremble: for the day of Jehovah cometh, for it is nigh at hand;*

[2] a day of darkness and gloominess, a day of clouds and thick darkness, as the dawn spread upon the mountains; a great people and a strong; there hath not been ever the like, neither shall be any more after them, even to the years of many generations.

[3] A fire devours before them; and behind them a flame burns: the land is as the garden of Eden before them, and behind them a desolate wilderness; yea, and none hath escaped them. (**This is a picture of the redeemed saints warring at the battle of Armageddon**).

[4] The appearance of them is as the appearance of horses; and as horsemen, so do they run.

[5] Like the noise of chariots on the tops of the mountains do they leap, like the noise of a flame of fire that devours the stubble, as a strong people set in battle array.

[6] At their presence **the peoples** *are in anguish; all faces are waxed pale.* (**The people here are the antichrists armies that had invaded Israel**).

⁷ They run like mighty men; they climb the wall like men of war; and they march every one on his ways, and they break not their ranks. **(We will march and conquer the enemies of Jesus and Israel.)**

⁸ Neither doth one thrust another; they march every one in his path; and they burst through the weapons, and break not off their course. **(The antichrist' army will shoot the saints, but it will not harm them in any way.)**

⁹ They leap upon the city; they run upon the wall; they climb up into the houses; they enter in at the windows like a thief.

¹⁰ The earth quakes before them; the heavens tremble; the sun and the moon are darkened, and the stars withdraw their shining.

*¹¹ **And Jehovah utters his voice before his army;** for his camp is very great; for he is strong that executes his word; for the day of Jehovah is great and very terrible; and who can abide it?* **(Once again Jesus is referred to as Jehovah, proving again His divinity.)**

Joel 3:2 *I will gather all nations and bring them down to the Valley of Jehoshaphat. There I will enter into judgment against them. Concerning my inheritance, my people Israel, for they scattered my people among the nations **and divided up my land.*** **(America had better leave Israel's land alone! God will defend her so don't let anyone touch the apple of His eye!)**

Zep 3:8 *Therefore **wait for Me, says Jehovah,** for the day I rise up to the prey; for My judgment is to gather the nations, for Me to collect the kingdoms, to pour on them My fury, all My hot anger. For all the earth shall be burned up with the fire of My jealousy.*

Joel 3:9-16

Proclaim this among the nations:
Prepare for war! Rouse the warriors!
Let all the fighting men draw near and attack.
¹⁰Beat your plowshares into swords and your pruning hooks into spears.
(God is calling them to come and be judged at the battle of Armageddon. That day even the fearful will feel brave and want to destroy Israel. It is Gods' will that they come.)
Let the weakling say, "I am strong!" **(Even the weak will feel strength to fight.)**

11Come quickly, all you nations from every side, and assemble there. **(There means the valley of Megiddo, called Armageddon, the designated place of battle.)**

Bring down your warriors, O Lord! **(Now the other army is mentioned, the Lords army. He said, bring DOWN, meaning they come from heaven.)**
12"Let the nations be roused; let them advance into the Valley of Jehoshaphat, **(Also known as the valley of Megiddo; Armageddon in the Greek)**

For there I will sit to judge all the nations on every side. (I have not spent any time discussing this, but the nations will either survive or be destroyed based on this judgment. If Jesus decides that they should not survive, then fire will fall on them.)
13Swing the sickle, for the harvest is ripe.
Come; trample the grapes, for the winepress is full
And the vats overflow--so great is their wickedness!"
As satan's followers have attempted to tread out the people of God, now God will trample them under foot.
14Multitudes, multitudes in the valley of decision!

For the day of the Lord is near in the valley of decision. **(The valley of decision is a fitting name for what happens here. Every nation will receive judgment based on Jesus' decision.)**
15The sun and moon will be darkened, and the stars no longer shine.
16The LORD (Jehovah in Heb., which again speaks of Jesus as Jehovah God.) **will roar from Zion and thunder from Jerusalem; the earth** *and the sky will tremble.* **(All the world will know that Jesus has returned. It will not be a secret anywhere).**
But the Lord will be a refuge for his people,
a stronghold for the people of Israel.
Two things to notice here; number one, Jesus is the leader and He destroys most of the antichrist' army. Number two, we are also riding on the horses of Heaven with Him and we also fight in this great battle.

It is not the angels who run thru the city and leap over the walls; it is us, the redeemed believers who return to this earth to reign with Jesus for one thousand years!

As the armies of the Lord pour out of Heaven the demonic spirits will cause the antichrist' armies to fire on them. The battle will last for a very short while. Jesus will personally destroy most of them with the sword that proceeds from His mouth. All we will do is chase after the remnants in the countryside and cities of Israel. By leading them to Megiddo the devil has laid all his cards on the table. It was his one chance. To defeat God he had to defeat and destroy every last Jew. As long as even one lived he could never be sure of victory.

In his madness and insanity the Mahdi antichrist will turn against the heavenly army. There will be no chance of his defeating even one member of that army yet he will try because he is demon possessed.

The false Jesus will surely be shocked when he sees the real Jesus Christ coming out of Heaven followed by the armies of God! This will not even be a close contest. Jesus will destroy the enemy quickly. The false version of Jesus and the antichrist Mahdi will realize too late that they have been tricked by the devil. They will not have time to repent. Theirs is a quick and decisive judgment. Hell awaits them and their followers.

WHAT HAPPENS TO THE DEMON SPIRITS AFTER JESUS COMES BACK?

Just as the devil will be bound, the demon spirits will also be bound. When Jesus was casting demon spirits out of people, they would beg Him to not torment them before the time. What they knew was that they were going to receive a definite punishment sometime in the future. The shamans and spiritualist in the world, as well as the psychics all are used of the demon spirits. On that day every last devil will be cast into the pit, called "abusso" in the Greek. It is a bottomless pit.

Luke 8:31 *And they begged Him that He would not command them to go out into the **abyss**.*

Mat 8:29 *And behold, they cried out, saying, what have we to do with thee, thou **Son of God**? Art thou come hither to torment us before the time?*

Jesus knew and the devils knew that He was going to punish them at a set time in the future. The devil lies and pretends that he can win, but he knows that judgment and justice await him; his end is certain.

Mat 25:41 *Then shall he say also unto them on the left hand, Depart from me, ye cursed, **into everlasting fire, prepared for the devil and his angels.*** At some point in the distant past God created hell with the clear understanding that it was created for the devil and his angels. He never made it for man. Man was intended to enter into the Glory of the Lord, not hell.

Isaiah 24:21 *And it shall come to pass in that day,* ***that the LORD shall punish the host of the high ones that are on high,*** *and the kings of the earth upon the earth .* **Eph 6:12**

Isaiah 24:22 ***And they shall be gathered together, as prisoners are gathered in the pit, and shall be shut up in the prison,*** *and after many days shall they be visited.* All of the demons will be locked up along with the devil.

WHAT HAPPENS TO THE ANTICHRIST AND THE FALSE PROPHET? - THEY ARE CAST ALIVE INTO HELL

Dan 7:11 *I beheld at that time because of the voice of the great words which the horn spoke; I beheld even till the beast was slain, and its body destroyed, and it was given to be burned with fire.* **(The antichrist and false prophet are taken alive, sentenced and then killed and thrown bodily into hell)**

Revelation 19:19-21 (ASV)

19 (ASV) And I **saw the beast,** *and the kings of the earth, and their armies, gathered together to make war against him that sat upon the horse, and against his army.*
20 And the ***beast was taken, and with him the false prophet*** *that wrought the signs in his sight, wherewith he deceived them that had received the mark of the beast and them that worshipped his image:* ***they two were cast alive into the lake of fire that burneth with brimstone:***
21 and the rest were killed with the sword of him that sat upon the horse, even the sword which came forth out of his mouth: ***and all the birds were filled with their flesh.***

Mat 25:31 *When the Son of man shall come in his glory, and all the holy angels with him, then shall he sit upon the throne of his glory.*

Mat 25:32 *And before him shall be gathered all nations: and he shall separate them one from another, as a shepherd divides his sheep from the goats.*

Mat 25:33 *And he shall set the sheep on his right hand, but the goats on the left.*

This judgment, **the judgment of the nations** will be the deciding factor on whether or not a person will be allowed to enter into the Millennium or not. Jesus will sit as a perfect judge and His judgment will be final with no appeals court to overturn it.

Gog And Magog After The War

Ezekiel 39:9-15 *and the inhabitants of the cities of Israel shall go out and shall set on fire and burn the weapons, both the shields and the bucklers, the bows and the arrows, and the javelins, and the spears. And they shall burn them with fire seven years,* (this means that there will be millions of people attacking. For Israel to be using the pieces of wood seven years later would mean an enormous army had come.) **39:10** *so that they shall take no wood out of the field, nor cut down any out of the forests for they shall burn the weapons for fire. And they shall plunder those who plundered them, and rob those who robbed them, says the Lord Jehovah. 39:11 And it will be in that day I will give to Gog a place there, a grave in Israel, the valley of those who pass by, east of the sea. And it shall stop the noses of those who pass by. And there they shall bury Gog and his entire multitude. And they shall call it, The Valley of the Multitude of Gog.* (For those who insist that these people are destroyed by a nuclear weapon I simply ask, "why isn't the ground radioactive? How can these other people simply be passing thru? If it was radioactive they couldn't")

39:12 *and the house of Israel shall bury them, to cleanse the land, seven months.* Verse 14 says at the end of seven months.

39:13 ***and all the people of the land shall bury.*** (Once again I want to appeal to common sense; **all the people** would not be able to spend their time burying the armies of Gog during the tribulation. The antichrist would have attacked them if they were that involved. This is clearly **after the tribulation** that God is speaking about). *And it shall be a name to them,* ***the day when I am glorified,*** *says the Lord Jehovah.* (Most prophecy teachers insist that this passage only refers to the war at the beginning of the tribulation period. However if you compare the scriptures you will see that they line up exactly with the rest of the

Bible concerning the Day of the Lord which occurs at the Battle of Armageddon. This is no coincidence.)

39:14 *And men shall separate those who continually pass through the land, burying those who passed through*(during the Tribulation it would be nearly impossible for Israel to have its' people passing thru the area of Megiddo and the Bekka valley burying people, especially millions of people.)

<u>Who remain on the face of the earth</u>, (The language makes it clear that not many will remain. This is after the tribulation.)

To cleanse it. (There is no cleansing of the land during the tribulation.) *At the end of seven months they shall search.* At the end of seven months would definitely mean after the battle of Armageddon. Since no where during the tribulation does Israel have the respite it would require to perform the burying, again I have to point out the obvious; this is after the tribulation.

39:15 *And as they pass, those who pass through the land, and any man sees a bone, then he shall build a post beside it, until the buriers have buried it in The Valley of the Multitude of Gog.* There are many who insist that these bones of Gog are radioactive and that this battle happens at the beginning of the Tribulation Period. There is no reason to teach that based on comparative scripture studies. For instance, in verse 13 it clearly says that it will be **the day when God is glorified**. There is only one day that is called this in the Old Testament and that is at the battle of Armageddon.

There is no scriptural reason to believe that Israel will be burning their enemies' weapons during the Tribulation. Why would they? There would be every reason to keep them in case of another attack. From studying the book of Revelation it is clear that the antichrist is very active during the time of the Tribulation. Israel would never be at peace enough to destroy every weapon or to hire men to be grave diggers in the area of Golan and the Bekka Valley.

The second half of the tribulation will be a time of constant warfare. Even if the two witnesses killed the armies of Gog and Magog in the beginning of the Tribulation, they would not need nuclear weapons. So common sense dictates that this is not a nuclear attack that kills the enemy.

Furthermore God clearly says that Gog and Magog come up in the **Last Days**. Every passage about the battle of Armageddon agrees with **Ezekiel 37, 38 & 39.** I know this will cause many to disagree with me, but the Bible clearly agrees with what I have said. Or better yet, I agree with the Bible.

Chapter thirteen

The One Thousand Year Reign Of Jesus Christ On This Earth

THE MILLINEUM. Latin; MILLI-1,000; ANUM-year.

It will be the saints' duty to rule over the cities and towns of this world alongside Jesus, the supreme ruler. There will be no elections. Jesus will rule justly but with a rod of iron. His decisions will be final. There will be no evil spoken of, printed, or broadcast any more. As the redeemed of the Lamb, we will not be tempted to sin any more. There will be no desire for fame or fortune. We will reign justly, because our great redeemer governs thru us. Every village and settlement on earth will either accept His rule or perish. There will be no opposition party. No debates. No commercials opposing the Word of God. No abortions. No racism. Everyone will work. The earth will be blessed and the curse on the soil will be gone. The land will bring forth bountifully to everyone who sows in it.

Zec 14:16-21 *And it shall be, everyone who is left of all the nations which came up against Jerusalem shall go up from year to year to worship the King,* **Jehovah of Hosts**, *and to keep the Feast of Tabernacles.*
And it shall be whoever will not come up from all the families of the earth to Jerusalem to worship the King, Jehovah of Hosts, **even on them shall be no rain.** *And if the family of Egypt does not go up, nor come in, they shall have no rain, but the plague with which Jehovah shall strike the nations who do not come up to keep the Feast of Tabernacles. This shall be Egypt's offense, and the offense of all the nations who do not come up to keep the Feast of Tabernacles.* (The Lord Jesus is again referred to as Jehovah. If any nation refuses to come up to Jerusalem to worship Jesus they will get no rain.)

*In that day there shall be on the bells of the horses, **HOLY TO JEHOVAH.** And the pots in Jehovah's house shall be like the bowls before the altar. Yea, every pot in Jerusalem and in Judah shall be **holy to Jehovah of Hosts.***

Mic 7:19 *He will turn again; He will have pity on us. He will trample our iniquities. **Yea, you will cast all their sins into the depths of the sea.***

Amos 9:14 *And I will bring again the captivity of my people of Israel, and they shall build the waste cities, and inhabit them; and they shall plant vineyards, and drink the wine thereof; they shall also make gardens, and eat the fruit of them.*

Amos 9:15 *And I will plant them upon their land, and they shall no more be pulled up out of their land which I have given them, saith the LORD thy God.* Thus all Israel will be saved; **Romans 11:26.**

Oba 1:17 *But upon Mount Zion shall be those who escaped; and it shall be holy. And the house of Jacob shall possess their own possessions.* God will keep His word that He spoke to Abraham. Israel will always live in the Promised Land. It is theirs by covenant treaty signed by God.

Amos 9:11-14

In that day will I raise up the tabernacle of David that is fallen, and close up the breaches thereof; and I will raise up his ruins, and I will build it as in the days of old (Jesus is the seed of David. He will sit on David's throne as King of kings and Lord of Lords. *12That they may possess the remnant of Edom,* (the area of ancient Edom is the Sinai Peninsula) *and of all the heathen, which are called by my name,* (all the world has heard of Jesus, but will not accept Him until He returns) *saith the LORD that doeth this.*

13Behold, the days come, saith the LORD, that the plowman shall overtake the reaper, and the treader of grapes him that soweth seed; (There will be so much food that no one will go hungry. The entire earth will bring forth such a vast amount of produce that it will grow faster than men can reap it.)

And the mountains shall drop sweet wine, (This means that grapes will be bursting before people can harvest them. The hills will literally flow with juice.) *And all the hills shall melt. 14And I will bring again the captivity of my people of Israel, and they shall build the waste cities, and inhabit them; and they shall plant vineyards, and drink the wine thereof*

(The Hebrew word for wine here is "aw-sees" which means fresh grape juice)'; *they shall also make gardens, and eat the fruit of them.*

Isaiah 11:6-9 *Also the wolf shall dwell with the lamb, and the leopard shall lie down with the kid; and the calf and the lion cub and the fatling together; **and a little child shall lead them**.*
And the cow and the bear shall feed; their young ones shall lie down together; and the lion shall eat straw like the ox.
And the suckling child shall play on the hole of the asp, and the weaned child shall put his hand on the adder's den.
*They shall not hurt nor destroy in all My holy mountain; **for the earth shall be full of the knowledge of Jehovah, as the waters cover the sea.***
Rev 20:6 *Blessed and holy is he that hath part in the first resurrection: on such the second death hath no power, but they **shall be priests of God and of Christ, and shall reign with him a thousand years.*** (We are promised that we will be a kingdom of priest; kings and priest.)

Exodus 19:6

*And you shall be to Me **a kingdom of priests** and a holy nation.' (Gods' desire has always been to make His people holy so that they could fellowship with Him.)*
1 Peter 2:9 *But you are a chosen generation, **a royal priesthood,** a holy nation, His own special people, **that you may proclaim the praises of Him who called you out of darkness into His marvelous light;***
Rev. 5:10 *And have made us **kings and priests** to our God;*
And we shall reign on the earth."
Most Christians don't know this, but they will not be in Heaven for ever. The Bible plainly tells us that we shall reign WITH CHRIST on this earth. Of all the prophecies that Christians love to quote, none seem to be as misquoted as the ones concerning the 1,000 year reign of Christ. Let me summarize what the Bible says will happen.

First, Jesus is coming back to stay on the earth for 1,000 years where He will rule the world with a rod of iron. All rebellion will be punished immediately.

Second, we will reign with Him as a reward. *"You have been faithful over a little, I will make you ruler over much"*, **Matthew 25:21.** We are promised that we will live and reign with Christ Jesus on this earth for 1,000 years. It will be during this same period of time that the devil will be locked up.

1 Cor. 6:2-3 *Do you not know that the saints will judge the world? And if the world will be judged by you, are you unworthy to judge the smallest matters? 3Do you not know that we shall judge angels? How much more, things that pertain to this life?*

For the Christian who can't seem to make a decision on their own it is hard to imagine being given leadership. But we forget that we will also have redeemed minds. We have the mind of Christ. He will guide us.

Isaiah 2:2-4 *in the last days the mountain of the Lord's temple will be established as chief among the mountains;*
It will be raised above the hills, **and all nations will stream to it.**
3Many peoples will come and say, "Come; let us go up to the mountain of the Lord, to the house of the God of Jacob. He will teach us his ways, so that we may walk in his paths." The law will go out from Zion, the word of the Lord from Jerusalem. (Jerusalem will be the world capital. All nations will send representatives to Israel or pay the consequences.)
4He will judge between the nations and will settle disputes for many peoples. (No one will be allowed to interpret law for himself anymore. The saints will hear from the Lords' mouth and relay that word to the people. Any who disagree will pay an immediate price for their rebellion.) ***They will beat their swords into plowshares and their spears into pruning hooks. Nation will not take up sword against nation, nor will they train for war anymore.*** (What the Lord is saying here in Isaiah is that He will actually stay in Jerusalem and that everyone will be able to see Him during the 1,000 years reign.)

Isaiah 65:18-25

18But be glad and rejoice forever in what I will create,
for I will create Jerusalem to be a delight and its people a joy.
19I will rejoice over Jerusalem and take delight in my people;
the sound of weeping and of crying will be heard in it no more.
20"Never again will there be in it an infant who lives but a few days, (**No more sorrowing over a lost child**) *or an old man who does not live out his years;*

He who dies at a hundred will be thought a mere youth; **(100 will be considered a very young age)**
He who fails to reach a hundred will be considered accursed.
21They will build houses and dwell in them; they will plant vineyards and eat their fruit.
22No longer will they build houses and others live in them,
or plant and others eat.
For as the days of a tree, so will be the days of my people ;(**An oak can live for over 200 years)**
my chosen ones will long enjoy the works of their hands.
23They will not toil in vain or bear children doomed to misfortune ;(**the blessing of total peace will be upon us)**
For they will be a people blessed by the LORD,
They and their descendants with them.
24Before they call I will answer;
while they are still speaking I will hear. (The Lord will be so close to His chosen people! Some have the idea that Jesus will **just be sitting** on a throne during the 1,000 years. Nothing could be further from the truth. **He will be totally involved** in the lives of His people.)
25The wolf and the lamb will feed together,
and the lion will eat straw like the ox,
but dust will be the serpent's food.
They will neither harm nor destroy
on all my holy mountain," saith the Lord.

What a wonderful picture of the Millennium is painted by the Lord. The Lord Jesus here is shown as a loving Shepherd watching over his flock. He is looking out for ways to bless and please those He loves.

Joel 3:17-21

"Then you will know that I, the LORD your God,
dwell in Zion, my holy hill. **LORD** here is Jehovah.
Jerusalem will be holy; never again will foreigners invade her.
18"In that day the mountains will drip new wine,
and the hills will flow with milk;
all the ravines of Judah will run with water.
A fountain will flow out of the LORD's house

and will water the valley of acacias. **(Ezekiel 47)**
20Judah will be inhabited forever and Jerusalem through all generations.
*21**Their bloodguilt, which I have not pardoned,
I will pardon.**" The* LORD *dwells in Zion!*

Jesus is repeatedly referred to as Jehovah in the prophets. There is no doubt that He is Jehovah God.

The Lord Jesus will crush the Islamic armies that are attacking Israel. Millions of unbelievers will be destroyed in a moment's time by the sharp sword that proceeds out of His mouth. The surviving Jews will witness what they have always wanted to believe about their Messiah, that He would come to fight and to deliver their nation.

Isaiah 4:2-6 *in that day shall the branch of Jehovah be beautiful and glorious, and the fruit of the land shall be excellent and comely for them that are escaped of Israel.* (Although many will die in the war of Armageddon, many will survive to see the Lord.)

*And it shall come to pass, that he that is left in Zion, and he that remaineth in Jerusalem, **shall be called holy,** even every one that is written among the living in Jerusalem;* (Every survivor will be called Holy.)

When the Lord shall have washed away the filth of the daughters of Zion, and shall have purged the blood of Jerusalem from the midst thereof, by the spirit of justice, and by the spirit of burning. (Jesus will literally save the nation in a day.)

*And Jehovah will create over the whole habitation of mount Zion, and over her assemblies, **a cloud and smoke by day, and the shining of a flaming fire by night**; for over all the glory shall be spread a covering.* (Just as the Spirit of the Lord abode over the camp of Israel in the Exodus, the Glory of the Lord will abide over the entire city of Jerusalem during the millennium.)

And there shall be a pavilion for a shade in the day-time from the heat, and for a refuge and for a covert from storm and from rain.

The remnant of Israel will be purified. God will drive away any doubts that they ever had about His love for them. Jesus will show them that the Lord is indeed their Shepherd.

The nation of Israel will be saved in a day.

Zech. 12:10 *"And I will pour out on the house of David and the inhabitants of Jerusalem a spirit of grace and supplication. **They will look on me, the one they have pierced,** and they will mourn for him as one mourns for an only child, and grieve bitterly for him as one grieves for a firstborn son.*

Zec 13:6 *And one shall say to him, **What are these wounds in your hands?** Then he shall answer, **Those with which I was wounded in the house of those who love Me.***

What a shock it will be for the Jews to see Jesus as He really is. For them to find out that it was Jesus who was their Messiah 2,000 years ago and they didn't know it. What will it be like to actually come up to Him after the battle is over and to touch His hands?

I believe the shock of knowing what happened to the Son of God will be numbing. Not only were they mistaken about the Christians, they didn't even understand their own prophets. They completely missed the truth of Jesus!

Jesus will come into the city and truly purify it. All over the earth the wild animals will suddenly settle down. Viruses that kill now will become totally harmless then. Pollution will be healed instantly. Cancer will disappear in an instant.

There will be no sickness, no disease. There will be no anger or hatred anymore. Peace will be the law of the land. No one will steal anything. Your valuables will be safe. No one will need to lock their doors. No dog will attack or even bark at you. No mosquito will bite, nor bee sting ever again.

One thousand years of peace, where the snake and lion will cease to hunt the prey and everyone on earth will be at peace. They will not even teach warfare for one thousand years.

People will survive the tribulation and the battle of Armageddon. For one thousand years these people will be ruled by Jesus Christ and there will be no sickness or still born babies. Extreme long life will enable the world to populate into the billions in a short time span. The earth will produce even in desert places. No people on earth will ever go hungry. No baby will have a head cold or fever. No old person will have arthritis. Jesus will cause the world to bloom. Peace will rule over every house and village. There will be no murders or rapes. Crime will be a forgotten thing. All disputes will be settled quickly by those redeemed followers of the Lamb who have accompanied Him from heaven.

Jerusalem will be the capital of the world. Every year all people will be required to come to Jerusalem to worship. The bible says if a nation doesn't come to worship it will get no rain. As much as we want to see the Lords return to earth, His reign will be over unredeemed men. Therefore they will grow resentful of having to do as they are told.

The devil is loosed for a short time after the 1,000 years

Revelation 20:1-3

1(ASV) And I saw an angel coming down out of heaven, having the key of the abyss and a great chain in his hand.
2 And he laid hold on the dragon, the old serpent, which is the Devil and Satan, and bound him for a thousand years,
*3 and cast him into the abyss, and shut it, and sealed it over him, that he should deceive the nations no more, **until the thousand years should be finished:** after this he must be loosed for a little time. **Rev 20:7** and when the thousand years are finished, Satan shall be loosed out of his prison, **Rev 20:8** and shall come forth to deceive the nations Which are in the four corners of the earth, Gog and Magog, to gather them together **to the war:** the number of whom is as the sand of the sea.*

How will the devil be able to deceive the people again? The same way that he has been doing it since time began.

1John 2:16 *because all that is in the world, the lust of the flesh, and the lust of the eyes, and the pride of life, is not of the Father, but is of the world.* He used all three areas to tempt Eve. **The lust of the eyes**; the fruit was good to look at. **The pride of life**; it would make you wise. **The lust of the flesh**; you will be like God.

These are the same areas that he tempted Christ with. **The lust of the flesh**; turn these stones to bread. **The lust of the eyes**; I will give You all these riches You see if You will only worship me. **The pride of life;** jump off the temple, God will not let You get hurt, You are special.

These are the exact same methods that the devil uses on all people. He has studied us for thousands of years. He knows what he is doing.

Eve fell for his lies but Jesus saw thru them. The people who will be alive at the end of the Millennium will be eager to hear what the devil says. One thousand years of living in peace will not stop the sin nature in man from wanting its way.

Rev 20:7 *and when the thousand years are finished, Satan shall be loosed out of his prison,* (God gives man choice. It is up to every person to decide what he will do with Jesus. Will he ignore Him? Rebel against His authority? Or will man accept Jesus as Lord?

It is up to every man to make up his own mind, choice is a gift from God but it carries much responsibility)

Rev 20:8 *and shall come forth to deceive the nations.* I believe that the devil will use the same exact tactic on these people that he used on Eve. The way he tricked Eve was to question Gods motive for keeping them from the tree of life. By putting doubt in their hearts and making them believe that God doesn't want them to have what they feel they should have rebellion is assured.

It wasn't that God was keeping something good from Adam and Eve. He was saving them from something very bad. Death itself is not as bad as being separated from Gods presence. The people who rebel against Jesus after the thousand years will surely be acting out of pride. They will feel that they have been held back and will want to rule themselves. This will be the last chance for man.

For every atheist the argument is "if there really is a God, why does He allow pain and suffering?" What they are really saying is that without pain and suffering they might believe in God, but because there is pain they won't. Jesus will rule for one thousand years during which there will be no pain, sickness, or even a bug bite. What is the net result? Man rebels anyhow.

Rev 20:9 *and they went up over the breadth of the earth, and compassed the camp of the saints about, and the beloved city:*

(After one thousand years of peace, rebellion is still in mans heart. We try to blame the devil for all of our sins, but the heart of man is exceedingly wicked on its own.)

162

And fire came down out of heaven, and devoured them. (Once again the devil brings his armies to Jerusalem, only this time God sends fire and destroys them all in an instant)

Rev 20:10 ***And the devil that deceived them was cast into the lake of fire and brimstone, where also the beast and the false prophet ARE; and they shall be tormented day and night for ever and ever.*** For those who insist that sinners will suffer for a short time, here the Bible makes it plain that they will suffer forever and forever. It is torment that they feel. Also notice that the beast and the false prophet have been here for a thousand years and are still alive. The word says, ***"Where the beast and false prophet ARE",*** **and** ***"forever and forever".***

Why would God allow the devil to deceive people who have been born long after the devil was locked up and have never known sin? Because all people have to make a conscious choice about Jesus.

No one gets saved by accident; you have to make the choice yourself to accept Him or to reject Him. The choice is yours.

Many can not accept that Jesus would allow the devil to run around on His earth. They must understand that man has always had the ability to tell the devil no. He also has always had the responsibility to resist the devils' schemes. Unfortunately man normally agrees with the devil far more often than he agrees with God. This is why we have so many problems in the world today. It isn't Gods' fault; it is mans. Choice is a powerful tool, or it is a dangerous weapon. The difference is the person who uses it.

The great white throne Judgment of sinners

Rev 20:11 *And I saw a great white throne, and him that sat upon it, from* ***whose face the earth and the heaven fled away;*** *and there was found no place for them.*

Rev 20:12 *And I saw the dead, the great and the small, standing before the throne;* ***and books were opened:*** *and another book was opened, which is the* ***Book of Life: and the dead were judged out of the things which were written in the books, according to their works.*** **(The Christian is judged according to what they have done in the body. The sinners are here judged according to everything they have ever done. The books are the Book of Life, and the Bible. Psalms 119:89**

163

forever, O Jehovah, Thy word is settled in heaven. **The Word of God is eternal, never changing. He has preserved it in Heaven and it has not changed.)**

Rev 20:13 *and the sea gave up the dead that were in it; and death and Hades gave up the dead that were in them:* ***and they were judged every man according to their works.***

Rev 20:14 *and death and Hades were cast into* ***the lake of fire.*** *This is the second death,* ***even the lake of fire.*** **(It is hard for people to imagine something worse than hell, but the lake of fire is worse. Even hell is cast into it.)**

Rev 20:15 *and if any was not found written in the book of life, he was cast into the lake of fire.* **(There is no appeals court. If your name is not written down, you will be cast into the lake of fire. The word which is translated "cast" means that someone (an Angel) will take you by their hands and toss you in.)**

Dan 7:9 *I beheld till thrones were placed, and one that was* ***Ancient of Days*** *did sit: his raiment was white as snow, and the hair of his head like pure wool; his throne was fiery flames, and the wheels thereof burning fire.* (This is reminiscent of John's picture of Jesus in the first part of the book of Revelation. He truly is the "Ancient of Days" because He is God, **Colossians 1:16-17.**

Dan 7:10 *a fiery stream issued and came forth from before him: thousands of thousands ministered unto him, and ten thousand times ten thousand stood before him: the judgment was set,* ***and the books were opened.*** There are two classes of people pictured here, those who minister to Him, and those who are judged by Him. Only the sinners will receive judgment.

Hell itself is cast into the lake of fire. This cleanses the earth's heart where hell is located. All sinners will have to answer for every sin. The Christian only answers for our works at the Bema seat judgment because all of our sins are forgiven. But the sinner still has every sin and their stains on their heart.

At the judgment there will be nothing left in any of these people that is Godly. All love and peace are gone. Kindness and joy are no longer in anyone's heart. **Only the most depraved emotions are left.** Anything that is remotely good will be taken away and replaced by remorse and fear. The maggots of hell fire never die. The heat never cools. Pain is always terrible. Loneliness is all that they have left. **If you are not saved then please get saved now.**

The lake of fire is a place of separation from the presence of God. That means that nothing kind or peaceful will be there. There will not be love there. It is a real place where real people will go. There will be weeping, loud crying pleading and begging to get out. There will be gnashing of teeth, pain so intense that they will grind their teeth. Also there will be no mercy there; no one will ever get out.

Chapter fourteen

New Heaven and the new Earth

Isaiah 65:17 *__Behold, I will create new heavens and a new earth.__ The former things will not be remembered, nor will they come to mind.*
Rev 21:1 *__Then I saw a new heaven and a new earth.__ The first heaven and the first earth disappeared, and the sea vanished.* (The sea will not be needed any more, neither will the moon or stars or sun. God will be the light of the world.) **2Pe 3:10** *but the day of the Lord will come as a thief; in the which the heavens shall pass away with a great noise, and the elements shall be dissolved with a fervent heat and the earth and the works that are therein shall be burned up.*
Rev 21:2 *And I saw the Holy City, the __New Jerusalem, coming down out of heaven from God__, prepared and ready, like a bride dressed to meet her husband.*
Rev 21:3 *I heard a loud voice speaking from the throne: __"Now God's home is with people!__ He will live with them, and they shall be his people. God himself will be with them, and he will be their God.* (This has always been God's desire, to be in and among His people. He wants to have communion with you.)
Rev 21:4 *He will wipe away all tears from their eyes. There will be no more death, no more grief or crying or pain. The old things have disappeared."* (This is wonderful; God Himself will reach out His hand and personally take the tears away from the eyes of all of His children.)
Rev 21:5 *then the one who sits on the throne said, "And now I make all things new!" He also said to me, "Write this, because these words are true and can be trusted."*
Rev 21:6 *and he said, "It is done! I am the first and the last, the beginning and the end. To anyone who is thirsty I will give the right to drink from the spring of the water of life without paying for it.*
John 7:37 *And in the last day of the great feast, Jesus stood and cried out, saying, __If anyone thirsts, let him come to Me and drink.__*

John 7:38 *He who believes on Me, as the Scripture has said, "Out of his belly shall flow rivers of living water."*

Rev 21:7 *<u>those who win the victory will receive this from me: I will be their God and they will be my children.</u>*

The parenting desire of God is seen again; He wants to be your Father. It is His greatest desire.

The earth will be purified before God steps foot on it or allows the New Jerusalem to come down to it. Earth will be as pure as Heaven. <u>New</u> in the Greek (**Rev.21:1**) means something that has been re-done, made new. It is not a picture of a completely new earth but of a renewed earth. All of the old is gone. Even hell is gone. No more stars in the sky or sun or moon. The only light that is in the new earth is the Lamb of God and God Himself.

The New Jerusalem. Revelation 21:10-21

John 14:2 **In my Father's house are many mansions: if it were not so, I would have told you. I go to prepare a place for you.**

John 14:3 *<u>And if I go and prepare a place for you, I will come again, and receive you unto myself; that where I am, there ye may be also.</u>*

John was taken away in the spirit to see the New Jerusalem coming from Heaven to the Earth. The description is so strikingly similar to the High Priest' breastplate that it can't be mere coincidence.

1. It is foursquare, just like the breastplate.
2. It has twelve stones, just like the breastplate.
3. It has the names of the twelve tribes of Israel, just like the breastplate.

Rev 21:19 *The first foundation, jasper ;(tribal color of Judah)*

The second, sapphire; (tribal color of Rueben)

The third, agate; (tribal color of Gad)

The fourth, emerald; (tribal color of Levi)

Rev 21:20 *the fifth, onyx; (tribal color of Joseph)*

The sixth, sardius; (tribal color of Simeon)

The seventh, chrysolite;(tribal color of Benjamin)

The eighth, beryl; (tribal color of Issachar)

The ninth, topaz; (tribal color of Nephtali)

The tenth, chrysoprasus; (tribal color of Zebulon)

The eleventh, jacinth ;(tribal color of Dan)
The twelfth, amethyst (tribal color of Asher)

The city has gates that are never closed. Only righteous people will live there. The earth will be filled with the knowledge of the glory of the Lord like the waters cover the seas, **Habakkuk 2:14.** The city is roughly 1,500 miles by 1,500 miles in width and height. It is a perfect square.

Billions and billions of people could live in it. There will be neither weariness nor boredom there. It will be on earth and God the Father and the Son will be on earth with us. Once again I want to remind you, we are not going to be in Heaven for eternity, we are going to be on this earth. **It will be the Breastplate of God, which will be the covering for His heart.**

In Ezekiel 28, Lucifer is seen to have 10 covering stones before he fell. 7 is the number of God's perfection, plus 3, the number of the triune God. The ruby, topaz, and the diamond, the beryl, the onyx, and the jasper, the sapphire, the turquoise, and the emerald, and gold were the stones that covered him as he led worship to God. Worship will be face to face! We will lead the worship of our God and King.

The River Of God

Zec 14:8 *and it shall come to pass in that day, **that living waters shall go out from Jerusalem;** half of them toward the eastern sea, and half of them toward the western sea: in summer and in winter shall it be.*
Rev 22:1 *and he showed me a **pure river of water of life,** clear as crystal, proceeding out of the throne of God and of the Lamb.*
Eze 47:1 *And he led me again to the door of the house. And behold, **water came out from under the threshold of the house eastward.** For the front of the house is east, and the water came down from under the right side of the house, at the south side of the altar.*
Rev 22:2 *In the midst of the street of it, and on either side of the river, was **there the tree of life,** which bare twelve manner of fruits, and yielded her fruit every month: and the leaves of the tree were for the healing of the nations.*
Ezekiel 47:12 *And all trees for food shall go up by the torrent, on its bank on this side, and on that side. Its leaf shall not fade, nor its fruit fail. It will bear by its months, because its waters come out from the sanctuary. And*

its fruit shall be for food, and its leaf for healing. It is obvious that John and Ezekiel are speaking of the same trees and the same river. The river comes from the throne of Christ in Jerusalem. It will heal the waters of the earth. For most people the thought of eating in the New Earth is hard to imagine. The thought is, "why would we need to?"

Eating out of need is all we know. Yet it is clear that God intended food to be an enjoyable experience. Once the curse is gone the bad effects of food will be gone also. We will eat for enjoyment, not because we are hungry.

The Curse Is Removed

Rev 22:3 *and there shall be no more curse:* (what are the effects of the curse on the earth? The soil and animals were cursed along with mankind. The earth brought forth thorns and weeds instead of produce fit to eat. Man has endured the curse on his labors and even childbirth is cursed. Our minds have been cursed and it is hard to imagine what it would be like to be free, but that day is coming!) *But the throne of God and of the Lamb shall be in it; and his servants shall serve him:* (**God has plans for us throughout eternity. We will not get bored in His presence!**

Eph 2:7: *that in the ages to come He might show the exceeding riches of His grace in kindness toward us in Christ Jesus.* (In the ages to come; literally means forever and ever He wants to surprise us with His exceeding goodness. He imagines great and wonderful things that He wants to do to you and for you.)

1Co 2:9: *but as it is written, Things which eye saw not, and ear heard not, and which entered not into the heart of man, whatsoever things God prepared for them that love Him.* (**I don't believe you can imagine eternity any more than you can understand the intellect of God. His imagination is limitless, so is His intelligence. How could you figure out eternity?**)

Rev 22:4 *and they shall see his face;* *and his name shall be in their foreheads.* (**It has always been Gods' desire to walk and to talk to man. Adam had it for a while, but we will have that closeness forever!**)

Rev 22:5 *and there shall be no night there*

Isaiah 49:10 *They shall not hunger nor thirst; nor shall the heat nor sun strike them; for He who has mercy on them shall lead them; even by the springs of water He shall guide them.*

Rev 22:5 continued; *and they need no candle, neither light of the sun; for the Lord God gives them light:*

1Ti 6:16 *who alone has immortality, dwelling in light which cannot be approached,*

22:5 continued; *and they shall reign for ever and ever.* Who shall reign? The saints shall reign!

How shall we reign over a perfect society? God and Jesus are actually there in person, how could we add anything to the conversation? God has a plan! If reigning simply means that I will be in the royal palace with Him then I will be satisfied!

Time is a created thing just like space is. In the new Heaven and Earth there will be no need for time. Forever and ever we will be in His presence. **Old things will never come to mind.** No past. No regrets. No fear. Only happiness, joy and peace forever. **Makes you want to get saved all over again!**

You will travel at the speed of thought. Just think about someone and you will be in their presence instantly. There is no way to describe what it will be like to have no fear and no regrets. The former thoughts and failures will be forgotten because of the constant flood of new and better things. The Spirit of God and the mind of Christ will make us know all things we ever wanted to know about God.

What is most wonderful about the New Earth is that nothing about the past will even come into mind. Think of it, never a sad or depressing day. Never having to worry about what someone else is thinking. No regrets about something you have done. That is what God has in store for those who love Him and His Son.

1John 3:1; *Behold what manner of love the Father has given us, that we should be called children of God.*(I don't believe we have ever understood or appreciated just what it means to be called "children of God.") *Therefore the world does not know us, because it did not know Him.* **Luke 12:32**

1John 3:2; *Beloved,* **now we are children of God,** *and it has not yet been revealed what we shall be. But we know that when He shall be revealed,* **we shall be like Him, for we shall see Him as He is.** (What does it mean to be like Him? he is always confident and happy. There is never any fear in His heart. He knows that the Father is always listening. There is so much about Him that we just can't imagine. But we know this, we shall be like Him!)

1Cor 13:12; *for now we see in a mirror dimly,* **but then face to face.** *Now I know in part,* **but then I shall fully know** *even as* **I also am fully known.** (How well does the Lord know you and me? Do you really believe that He knows everything there is to know about you? Then if He does it stands to reason that you and I have never surprised God. Maybe we have disappointed Him but never surprised Him. One day we will know Him the same way He now knows us; fully and completely.

Jer 1:5 *Before I formed you in the belly I knew you;* *and before you came forth out of the womb I consecrated you.*

Psalms 139:17-18 *how precious also are Your thoughts to me,* *O God!* *How great is the sum of them!* *If I should count them, they are more than the sand;* *when I awake, I am still with You.*

The end is only the beginning!
Eternity waits!

How to have eternal life. Repent of your sins. Accept Jesus as your Savior and Lord. Get into a good bible believing church and study the Word of God faithfully. And most importantly, love the Lord with all your being.

Romans 10:9 *because if thou shalt confess with thy mouth Jesus as Lord, and shalt believe in thy heart that God raised him from the dead, thou shalt be saved:*

Rev. 12:11 *And they overcame him because of the blood of the Lamb, and because of the word of their testimony; and they loved not their life even unto death.*

Romans 10:13 *for, Whosoever shall call upon the name of the Lord shall be saved.*

1. (The **flag of jihad;** Permission is granted to copy, distribute under the terms of GNU Free Documentation License on the **Jihad flag only**. All other contents of this book are protected.)

Printed in the United States
78141LV00003B/478-528